PRAISE FOR

Messy Truth

"The church desperately needs wise and winsome guides that can equip us to lavishly love LGBTQ people in the context of very real, very messy churches and ministries. Caleb Kaltenbach is one of those guides!"

—MICHELLE SANCHEZ, executive minister of
Make and Deepen Disciples at Evangelical Covenant Church

"In *Messy Truth,* you will grow in your compassion for and conversation with those in the LGBTQ community. Caleb Kaltenbach is a leader and pastor who fosters relationships without sacrificing conviction, and he will teach you to do the same."

—KYLE IDLEMAN, senior pastor of Southeast Christian Church

"As our churches and our world become increasingly polarized on the complicated issues of life, Caleb Kaltenbach's ideas are a welcome voice of warmth and biblical clarity. Without sacrificing principle, he brings the reader a grace-filled lens to view the difficulties we face, which also provides practical skills."

—JOHN TOWNSEND, PhD, *New York Times* bestselling author of
the Boundaries series

"Once again, Caleb Kaltenbach tackles this difficult subject with superbly well-balanced grace and truth. His sensitivity and empathy regarding the LGBTQ community is one to be modeled. A must-read for all Christians."

—BECKET COOK, author of *A Change of Affection*

"Many books discuss research and theories about loving people, but this book models how we can relentlessly love people and meet them where they're at so we can guide them to Jesus."

—EFREM SMITH, co-senior pastor of Midtown Covenant Church

"*Messy Truth* provides a most practical guide—through stories, conversations, and tips for church leaders and Christians to show mercy over judgment."

—DJ CHUANG, author of *MultiAsian.Church*

"*Messy Truth* is a timely wake-up call for the church. It offers a road map for staying faithful to Scripture and being empathetic and gracious toward people in the LGBTQ community and beyond."

—SEAN MCDOWELL, PhD, associate professor of apologetics at Talbot School of Theology

"Caleb teaches us the art of seeing people—people whom Jesus loves. In *Messy Truth,* we are given the tools to have healing and life-giving conversations that ultimately foster community and belonging for all people."

—ADRIANNA CERVANTES, youth and young-adult programming coordinator at Shepherd Church

"Caleb's application of Jesus's powerful formula of grace and truth gives us the guidance we need to move forward in a way that honors God and loves people."

—RANDY FRAZEE, pastor and author of *His Mighty Strength*

"Bringing wisdom and clarity to the most complicated of situations, *Messy Truth* helps churches and followers of Jesus advance their faith beyond their agenda. This book goes beyond making a point; it makes a difference!"

—RUSTY GEORGE, senior pastor of Real Life Church

"Very few people these days combine convictions about God's Word with the ability to unleash compassion for everyone. Likewise, very few people these days are calling the church to full commitment to truth and full commitment to grace. That's the lesson in this book."

—RAY JOHNSTON, senior pastor of Bayside Church and founder of Thrive

"In *Messy Truth,* you'll learn how to best point your LGBTQ friends to Jesus and help them connect in Christ-centered communities."

—JARRETT STEPHENS, senior pastor of Champion Forest Baptist Church

"I am often asked, 'Who's doing it right? Who is a model for relating to the LGBTQ community?' I point people to Caleb Kaltenbach, whose book *Messy Truth* helps the reader catch his vision for entering into sustained, authentic relationships and provides practical examples from his own life and principles for doing so."

—MARK YARHOUSE, professor at Wheaton College and director of Sexual and Gender Identity Institute

"*Messy Truth* is exactly what the church needs in order to navigate today's murky cultural and relational waters with biblical fidelity and love. It forges a better way for Christians to love God and our neighbors faithfully and well, not only in the matters that are the subject of the book, but in any we might face in a post-Christian world."

—KAREN SWALLOW PRIOR, research professor of English, as well as Christianity and Culture, at Southeastern Baptist Theological Seminary

"I was drawn in by Caleb's winsome approach through the entire book and found myself wanting to talk about it with others. Gather your leadership team and dig into this book together!"

—RICH BIRCH, author of *Church Growth Flywheel* and host of *unSeminary Podcast*

"With the wisdom of personal experience and the kindness of a pastor's heart, Caleb helps us to love better across the lines of difference while maintaining our convictions. More than this, he helps us see that it is not in spite of our faith that we love in this way, but because of it."

—SCOTT SAULS, senior pastor of Christ Presbyterian Church in Nashville, Tennessee

"*Messy Truth* will help you think through the challenge of living and relating to people who see and live in the world differently than you do."

—DARRELL BOCK, executive director for cultural engagement at Howard G. Hendricks Center for Christian Leadership and Cultural Engagement

"This book is filled with real-life, lived, and wrestled-down wisdom. Allow Caleb to be your guide to help you discern God's truth, grow in compassion, and be able to have a conversation with anyone."

—DANIEL IM, lead pastor at Beulah Alliance Church, podcaster, and author

"This book demonstrates why redemptive community is essential in helping others follow Jesus, and Caleb provides a biblical framework along with practical steps to reach people different from ourselves."

—RUTH MALHOTRA, public relations and communications specialist

"As a culture, we refuse to honor people we disagree with, pretend truth doesn't exist, or run screaming back to our echo chambers to find people who agree with us. *Messy Truth* gives us a framework to have the meaningful dialogue we so desperately need to foster."

—CAREY NIEUWHOF, host of the *Carey Nieuwhof Leadership Podcast* and author of *At Your Best*

"Like a handmade tapestry, *Messy Truth* masterfully weaves together truth and love across the fabric of its pages. Whether you're leading an entire congregation or the kids at home, this is just the tool you need to navigate the world we're in."

—RICKY JENKINS, senior pastor of Southwest Church

"Caleb once again embraces the messiness of engaging people and challenges the church's often-flawed reaction to LGBTQ individuals. By establishing us all as image bearers and being worthy of not only love and respect but also viewed as beings of value, the argument of right versus wrong easily changes to simply loving and being loved by a just God. This paradigm shift is truly effective only when we make it as a community and include those we disagree with."

—LESLI HUDSON-REYNOLDS, gender identity ministries at Posture Shift

"Conversations about faith and sexuality are at the forefront of our society. I don't know of many people more qualified than my friend Caleb to speak to how we can engage with grace and truth."

—ASHLEY WOOLDRIDGE, senior pastor of Christ's Church of the Valley

"Caleb shows us—with biblical intelligence, pastoral wisdom, and lots of experience—that being radically gracious does not mean we are taking a soft approach to truth. Truth is grace and grace is truth. If we're not being gracious, we're not actually being truthful."

—PRESTON SPRINKLE, president of the Center for Faith, Sexuality, and Gender

"Caleb speaks with conviction and compassion, upholding biblical truth while humanizing some of the most difficult conversations today's culture is having."

—DAVE DUMMITT, senior pastor of Willow Creek Community Church

"Caleb Kaltenbach is uniquely qualified to lead this challenging conversation around engaging LGBTQ individuals in authentic community within the church. In *Messy Truth*, he guides us with both biblically sound theology and compassionate real-world examples to a model that reflects both the love and justice of God's truth."

—GEOFF S. SURRATT, director of ReThink Leadership

"The way Caleb has taught us to expand our vision for love, to deepen our walks in grace in messy places, and to passionately pursue, love, and commit to God's church leaves me inspired and smarter."

—ALBERT TATE, co-founder and lead pastor of Fellowship Church

"Caleb Kaltenbach has produced a highly readable, incredibly insightful, and richly relevant work in *Messy Truth*. It is firmly biblically and theologically grounded, yet practical, as we have come to expect from him."

—SCOTT RAE, dean of faculty at Talbot School of Theology

MESSY TRUTH

MESSY TRUTH

HOW TO FOSTER COMMUNITY
WITHOUT SACRIFICING CONVICTION

CALEB KALTENBACH

Author of *Messy Grace*

WATERBROOK

Library of Congress Cataloging-in-Publication Data
Names: Kaltenbach, Caleb, author.
Title: Messy truth : how to foster community without sacrificing conviction / Caleb Kaltenbach.
Description: First edition. | [Colorado Springs] : WaterBrook, an imprint of Random House, a division of Penguin Random House LLC, [2021]
Identifiers: LCCN 2020054706 | ISBN 9780525654278 (trade paperback) | ISBN 9780525654285 (ebook)
Subjects: LCSH: Church work with sexual minorities. | Truth—Religious aspects—Christianity.
Classification: LCC BV4437.5 .K35 2021 | DDC 259.086/6—dc23
LC record available at https://lccn.loc.gov/2020054706

PRINTED IN THE UNITED STATES OF AMERICA ON ACID-FREE PAPER

waterbrookmultnomah.com

2 4 6 8 9 7 5 3 1

First Edition

SPECIAL SALES Most WaterBrook books are available at special quantity discounts when purchased in bulk by corporations, organizations, and special-interest groups. Custom imprinting or excerpting can also be done to fit special needs. For information, please email specialmarketscms@penguinrandomhouse.com.

To five friends who model the principles of Messy Truth:

Jason Caine

Rusty George

Lane Jones

Carey Nieuwhof

Drew Sherman

CONTENTS

PART 3: CONVERSATIONS WITH EVERYONE

AUTHOR'S NOTE

When I wrote *Messy Grace,* I wanted to discuss personal relationships between Christians and their LGBTQ family and friends. *Messy Truth* takes this to a whole new level, as it considers how people find and follow Jesus better in community rather than isolation. One-on-one personal relationships must be developed, but God uses those personal relationships to bring people into community. This book pleads with Christians of any background to make room for people not like them. I've tried to write a book that acknowledges the nuance of doctrine and life experiences in the midst of many relationships. My hope is that you will come to appreciate the tension between what is believed and what is best lived out in a redemptive community.

Please note that I have changed the names and personal details of many of the people whose stories I am telling in this book in order to disguise their identities.

MESSY
TRUTH

HOW FAR ARE YOU WILLING TO GO?

W hat should we do?" The question hung heavy in the air. Three days earlier, I preached at this church's weekend services. For weeks, I had been consulting with the church leaders. Now they and I looked at each other with confused expressions. I glared at the conference room whiteboard in hopes that ideas and words from previous discussions would help, but no silver-bullet answer could alleviate the ambiguity we all felt.

We discussed scenarios the group was facing and I tried to give guidance, but the circumstance that led to the "What should we do?" question was a next-level discussion.

You see, earlier that year, two married lesbian couples with young kids began attending the church. This would have sent shock waves through most churches, but this church already had attendees who identified in some way as LGBTQ. And the sense of welcome in the community was real. The church was ethnically diverse and multigenerational, and because the leaders encouraged dialogue, attendees held various biblical perspectives. So, despite the church's conservative stance on marriage, the two families felt a sense of belonging. They felt *loved*.

But after a few months of being in community in the church, the four women agreed that marriage was a covenant between God, one man, and one woman. They had approached a staff pastor and asked a hard question.

"Should we divorce or stay married?"

Perplexed, the staff member just stared at them. (This is one of those questions not covered in seminary.)

Breaking the awkward silence, one of the women continued, "We're not quite sure what to do. We decided to go to a staff member because we trust our leaders."

Another one of the women looked at the staff member and observed, "You're still not saying anything. Are you worried about us having sex? My wife and I don't even *have* sex anymore."

That revelation didn't simplify things. Trying to get back to the main point, they expanded on their original question. "If my wife and I divorce, can we keep living together, as long as we don't have sex?"

Finally, the staff member confessed that he needed to think about the situation and that he would pray with them. (Good move!)

The two families agreed to meet with him again after a couple of weeks. And that is how, one week later, I found myself in a conference room with that staff member, some of the other leaders on the team, and a whiteboard full of ideas that weren't really helping us figure out what we should do.

In all sincerity, I hadn't processed a circumstance like this particular one before. For a second I thought, *Maybe I can just start talking until they like something I say.* But, thankfully, as quickly as that idea arrived, it vanished. We were not here to gloss over the difficulty but rather to engage it.

Letting go of my desire to be an "expert," I began to ask questions, two of which immediately came to mind: "What does Scripture say about sexual intimacy and relationships?" and "What does it mean to be above reproach in this scenario?"

I was barely able to voice these questions before the first opinion hit.

"They should just divorce," said Sarah, one of the leaders.

"Huh?" I was a little caught off guard.

We were not here to gloss over the difficulty but rather to engage it.

"Di-vorce!" she stated louder. "Isn't that what the couples are asking about? It's simple."

"Is it?" I asked. "I'm not saying they should or shouldn't end their marriages, but the word *divorce* makes me wince."

"They aren't *really* married," she said as if she were pointing out the obvious.

My eyes widened. "Um, yes they are."

"Not in God's eyes," she quickly retorted.

"They're not in what you and I would call a 'traditional marriage,' but according to the government and their love for each other, they're married."

The reality sank in a little deeper as silence monopolized the room once again.

"Look," I said, addressing Sarah, "I'm not trying to debate with you or anyone else. Like you, I believe God created sex to be expressed in a marriage between one man and one woman."

More silence. "I'm not suggesting what these couples should or should not do," I continued. "I'm saying we should proceed with caution and conversation. These are people's lives."

Just then, a board member named Robert asked, "Should we use unbiblical methods to solve extra-biblical situations?"

Before we could dive deeper into that question, the children's pastor asked, "And what about the kids? They were adopted from the foster system. Should they be split between two homes when they've had stability for a few years?"

"Another good question," I commented.

Mark, a board member who had appeared uncomfortable most of the night, looked frustrated. He made the time-out signal with his hands. "Am I hearing what I think I'm hearing?"

Paul, the lead pastor, asked, "What are you hearing, Mark?"

"So far, Sarah's the only one who's on the 'truth' side of things," he said, pointing at Sarah, who was now looking at the table with uncertainty. "I understand the need for love. But are we really going to recommend that these women stay married?"

"No one's said that," Paul uttered.

Mark looked at me and asked, "Isn't that what we want? Grace *and* truth?"

WHAT IS TRUTH?

Before we go further into the story, let me ask you: *What would you do?* If you were in this meeting, what would you have suggested? How far would you be willing to go? Don't know? That's fine, because most of the time, I'm not sure either. But our discussion in the conference room wasn't about my personal beliefs. Our goal was to discover the truth about God's will in this scenario. And often, discerning truth and applying it are daunting tasks.

So, how do you define *truth*? My personal definition of truth is "what's accurate and real." Simple, short, sweet.

There are varying sources of, forms of, and perspectives on truth. People gain knowledge and truth in various ways:

- using our senses
- having innate knowledge (what we are born knowing)
- facing life experiences (achievements, failures, relationships)
- observing the characteristics of an object (for example, that the chair is orange with four legs)
- being taught, told, or demonstrated things by others

Along these same lines, Christians believe that people learn about God through *general revelation* (knowledge of truth and God from nature and learning from others) and *special revelation* (knowledge of truth and God from spiritual sources, such as the Bible, Jesus, and angels). Both general and special revelation communicate truth but do so in different ways.

The concept of *unquestionable truth* means truth is absolute, as it aligns with proven facts, trustworthy data, and science. For instance, two plus two equals four, and water in its basic form is H_2O. It's difficult to argue with this kind of truth. In some settings, there is *agreed-upon truth,* in which all or a majority of people agree on a belief, account of what happened, strategy, and so on. This type of truth is objective.

> My personal definition of *truth* is "what's accurate and real." Simple, short, sweet.

There's also truth that is more subjective. Each person lives by a set of ethics, morals, values, and beliefs developed through their relationships, experiences, and faith. These form a person's *worldview.* Just as beauty is in the eye of the beholder, some ideas can "become true" to people. For instance, Amy (my wife) believes cauliflower is tasty, while I'm sure it's from Satan. She's convinced that cauliflower pizza crust tastes just like regular pizza crust, but I'm certain that even entertaining such an idea insults good pizza! A better name for this kind of truth is *preference*.

Some people, like the philosopher Plato, wouldn't even acknowledge preference as a category of truth. He believed there was a difference between knowledge and opinion: you learn one and are convinced of the other. He viewed knowledge (what we might call truth) as possessing greater moral authority than opinion because one can make a case for and defend what has been learned.[1]

Remember that though my definition of truth is simple, our concepts of and interaction with truth are undoubtedly complex. More times than not, when people attempt to find truth in a circumstance, it's buried underneath preferences, emotions, opinions, traditions, and even lies. This is especially true regarding the junction of relationships, faith, and the LGBTQ reality. What do you do when there's a gap between your beliefs and feelings? How should you move forward when your convictions about sexuality run contrary to the opinions of friends and family? Where do you find strength to build solid relationships with people despite disagreements? How do you share Jesus with those who have been hurt by Christians? How do you discuss God's words in a society that might label you an extremist for doing so?

IS TRUTH MESSY?

Every day, ordinary people—conservatives, progressives, celebrities, politicians, religious leaders, and activists—post to social media their many opinions about life. When we blindly post about anyone or any community, we often forget that we're describing actual human beings with emotions and experiences. No wonder faith and LGBTQ conversations can be so complicated.

A great example of this mess is found in the literary world. After the conclusion of the Harry Potter series, author J. K. Rowling stated that a main character named Dumbledore (an older wizard who is a wise sage) was gay and used to be involved in a passionate relationship with someone who later became his enemy.[2] Of course, the internet lost its mind. Harry Potter fans had mixed feelings about Rowling's announcement. There were excited fans, indifferent fans, and offended fans. Many were annoyed that she defined aspects of Dumbledore's character after the series was completed. The fact that Dumbledore wasn't going to be portrayed as gay in the *Fantastic Beasts* movie franchise disappointed several fans.[3] Unfortunately, some voiced their disapproval with negative clichés that inappropriately judged anyone on the LGBTQ spectrum.

First, remember that Rowling is the author of the series. Regardless of anyone else's opinion, as the creator, she's entitled to say what she wants about her books and their characters. Second, negative catchphrases and buzzwords are not loving or necessary. They don't represent the majority of those who relate in some way as LGBTQ. People have depth, and it's dehumanizing to characterize a person's life, beliefs, and relationship decisions with simplistic negative phrases.

Yet the complexities of relationships, faith, sex, and the LGBTQ reality run deeper than literary series and hit movies. It's personal for all of us.

In my book *Messy Grace*, I share my story of being raised by two lesbians and a gay man. Having roots in their LGBTQ community, I was taught, "Christians hate gay people. If you are not like them, they will not like you." Because of that often all-too-true sentiment, it was challenging for me to see Jesus past the pseudo-Christians who protested pride parades, ignored their children dying of AIDS, and so on. I mean, how does an all-loving God have such hate-filled followers? I grew up thinking, *If Christians are this awful, I can't imagine how horrible Jesus must be.* But our feelings are no match for how Jesus loves people. I finally saw his love reflected in the way some believers lived their lives and treated me.

Eventually, I came out to my parents as a Christian. Let's just say that Mom, Dad, and Vera were less than thrilled. They basically kicked me out of their houses for a while. Several years later, some Christians in Dallas opened their arms to my parents, and they started following Jesus. Grace can certainly feel messy, right? The discrepancy between Jesus's love for people and legalists' contempt for my family made grace feel messy. Although grace *looks* and *feels* messy when it intersects with our messy lives, God's grace is anything but messy. In the same way, God's truth is perfect even though it may seem messy to us.

In Psalm 19:7–9, David described God's words as perfect, trustworthy, right, radiant, pure, and firm. Truth appears messy whenever God's words contradict my sinful desires and decisions.

Even though God's words are *not* messy or irrelevant, our feelings can lie to us and tell us otherwise. Emotions can be so loud that it's easy to regard them as true even when they are not. Those sinful emotions can seduce us into misinterpreting God's words, making them feel messy.

Truth *feels* messy when it

- creates conflict between our beliefs and emotions
- questions our decisions, ideas, habits, and plans
- challenges our morals, personal values, and theological convictions
- causes disagreement among family members
- initiates concern over a friend's decision
- necessitates tough conversations with someone we care about

Notice a commonality of why truth can feel messy? Our emotional attachments to people. The distinction between God's truth and our emotional attachments can tempt us to *perceive* truth as messy. In turn, we make unhealthy decisions like overreacting to circumstances, offering unsolicited opinions, and avoiding difficult conversations because we are scared of facing emotional pain.

It's completely normal to be afraid of hurting individuals we care for. No one wants to give the wrong impression, communicate their beliefs poorly, or lose relationships. You can relate, right? I know I can. But conceding to fear is far from healthy; it's spiritually lethal.

Toxic fear always diverts us from Jesus's mission: loving people well. It prevents us from embracing anyone unlike us or engaging in complicated situations. Fear can provoke us to ask unhelpful questions, such as "What's at stake if we engage?"

What's at stake if we walk alongside individuals we assume to be messy? What's at stake if we challenge others' opinions? What's at stake if we invite people to church or attempt to share Jesus with them? Such questions are never helpful, because they originate from fear. They focus on what we might potentially lose instead of what God and others stand to lose. It reveals our fixation on personal losses rather than on what others might gain. Posing the question "What's at stake if we engage?" is comparable to telling God, "Even though you'd get the glory if they followed you, don't use me as a catalyst for a pivotal moment in another person's life!"

> What's at stake if we *don't* engage?

Instead, maybe we should ask, "What's at stake if we *don't* engage?"

Asking this question takes the spotlight off us. If we don't engage, who will? If we refuse to take the mission of Christ seriously, who will?

What's at stake if we don't engage? The answer? People.

THE NECESSITY OF COMMUNITY

Before following Jesus, I attended a Bible study in a misguided attempt to prove Christianity wrong. I assumed every Christian was just like the ungodly "Christian" street protesters who treated my parents and their friends like trash. Make no mistake: I wanted to dismantle their faith. Little did I know how quickly my plans would crumble.

Despite my desire to bring down their Christian faith, I kept attending the Bible study, and in the summer before my junior year in high school, I trusted Jesus. Specifically, there were two primary reasons I decided to follow him.

First, I realized that Jesus was nothing like the street-corner pseudo-Christian protesters. He was unlike anything or anyone I had imagined. Those were some of the best days of my life. I couldn't wait to read the Bible before school, during class, after school, and even in the middle of the night. I wanted to learn as much as I could about Jesus and tell everyone about him. I took every opportunity to volunteer at my church and attend classes, and I joined the church's student ministry.

The community I experienced with these Christians afforded me the chance to discover Jesus, learn how to follow him, and figure out how to share my faith with others. It was a snapshot of truly authentic relationships, and I assumed most Christian communities were the same. At least that's what I thought until the following summer.

I had been a Christian for a year when a friend named Allie invited me to attend summer camp with her church's student ministry. Excited for another chance to meet new people and grow spiritually, I accepted her invitation. The first day of the camp was fantastic! I made some new friends and gained further insights about Jesus. That evening, new students were encouraged to share their testimonies by the campfire. I had a strong desire to tell my story, but I was nervous. Memories of people who protested my mom's parades were still fresh, but I was convinced that none of those angry fundamentalist tendencies resided in the people at this camp.

When we gathered for campfire time during the next evening, I mustered the courage to share my fledgling testimony. I didn't leave anything out: my parents' divorce, raised by two lesbians and a gay man, hating Christians and then trusting Jesus, and growing over the previous year. Although most of the students appeared fairly receptive, I later discovered that the student-ministry pastor and some of his volunteers were anything but compassionate.

The next morning, my cabin leader told me that the student-ministry pastor and a couple of the volunteers wanted to speak with me. I was only seventeen and completely oblivious to what was about to happen. I endured almost an hour of questions and a small lecture, none of which was appropriate: "Are you gay? Have you ever been with another guy? Are you attracted to any students at the camp? Do you think your parents are trying to recruit you? Why are you here? Why are you *really* here?"

Afterward, they prayed for me and cautioned me to be on my best behavior.

"We'll be watching," one of the volunteers told me.

It goes without saying that I decided to go home after the meeting. From that day forward, my friendship with Allie was okay at best. I'm still not certain what they told her, but in all likelihood, it wasn't good.

Rarely have I shared that story. Even today it's still painful. However, the experience changed my life in a good way! It taught me how to distinguish between unhealthy and healthy Christian community. Because I was attending a good church and Bible study, I understood that not all Christians were like those camp

> God used a bunch of messy people to reach a messy person like me.

leaders. My true community loved me even though my life was messy. The people from my church and Bible study comprised the second reason I trusted Jesus and kept following him. Even though I was messy, these believers

- showed kindness
- didn't expect perfection
- allowed me to disagree
- gave me margin to process life and faith
- owned their mistakes
- openly shared about their pain and doubt
- never got offended when I asked tough questions

One of the most important days of our lives is when we realize that God uses us to make a difference in the lives of others. The example of these Christian friends compelled me to drop my assumptions about and prejudice against Christians. I began to believe that God loved me despite my messiness because *they* loved me despite my messiness. God used a bunch of messy people to reach a messy person like me. Those relationships influenced me to start my lifelong journey of loving God and people.

FIGHTING FOR INFLUENCE

Since 2017, I've been helping churches, ministry organizations, and Christian learning institutions discover how to love and foster community with LGBTQ individuals without sacrificing theological convictions. Basically, I offer guidance in developing systems that allow anyone to attend while honoring the organization's doctrine and values. It's a blast to journey with leaders by assisting them in endeavors like training small-group leaders for every age level, working with staff teams, and developing policies with church boards.

Much of my time is spent in meetings or in coaching conversations with ministry leaders, pastors, all-star volunteers, attendees, and those who don't attend church. I've sat in living rooms crying with married couples, parents, and teenagers. I've pleaded with family members not to walk away from relationships regardless of how they view sexuality. I've tried to show people that loving others doesn't require a doctrinal shift on the subject of marriage. It's not unusual to find me meeting in a coffee shop with someone who has different views than I do. Ultimately, I believe our differences should be driving us to dialogue instead of dividing us.

Whether I'm strategizing with a pastor of a twenty-thousand-member church or fifty-member church, a small-group leader, a mom, a sibling, or whomever, people ask the same questions every time:

- "Do my biblical beliefs about marriage betray my friends?"
- "Is my church safe enough for me to invite my friend?"
- "What should I do if a family member came out to me and it didn't go well?"

Churches should want everyone to feel welcome. Students who have adopted gender-fluid pronouns need to feel loved by

Christians. The dad who confessed his attraction to men still needs community, and so does his family. First-time church guests in same-sex relationships shouldn't be asked to leave but instead should be encouraged to keep returning. Short of sinning, believers should be doing whatever is necessary to earn influence so they can point people to Jesus.

Influence is all about people. Having influence in another person's life is tremendously valuable. The more influence you have with someone, the more weight your words and actions carry. Influence can also help you answer questions that are emotionally complex.

For instance, people regularly ask me if they should attend the wedding of a loved one who is marrying someone of the same biological sex. I used to give reasons for both attending and not attending. However, now I ask them two questions. First, I ask, "If you didn't attend the wedding, would it cost you influence?"

Usually, they answer yes. Then I ask the second question: "What are you willing to do to keep and build influence with _____?"

Whoever's name is in the blank at the end of the second question usually determines their answer. Put yourself in their position for a moment to understand the depth of the dilemma. What if it's your son? Daughter? Spouse? Best friend? Sister? Nephew? Coach? How far would you go to be one of their first calls or texts when life punches them in the face? Are you okay with other Christians misinterpreting your efforts? Would you be satisfied with only God knowing the true intentions of your heart?

> "What are you willing to do to keep and build influence with _____?"

Your love for others is measured by what you will endure for them. Influence comes from relationships, and relationships can be strengthened in the midst of community. Influence is worth fighting for.

But how do you best earn influence? What does it look like to cultivate the kind of community that deepens relationships? How can your influence and community inspire people to follow Jesus?

THE MESSY PATH FORWARD

New Testament leaders such as John, Paul, and Peter understood a difficult yet simple principle: following Jesus doesn't spare us from the struggle of being fallen humans. If anything, Romans 7:14–25 confirms that Paul was well aware of his continued need to surrender, even while having a relationship with Jesus. If there was ever anyone that wasn't afraid to admit his messiness, it was Paul. We should adopt his authenticity, because *messy* refers to all of us.

The pages ahead contain stories of people who either relate to, identify as, or have experience with the LGBTQ reality. We're going to dive into the relational contours of faith, sexuality, conversations, and community. You may or may not appreciate some of the stories you're about to encounter. After finishing this book, you might believe that I went too far or didn't go far enough on certain topics or theological issues. I cannot force God's words to conform to our expectations, nor can I offer perfect solutions for every question

> Is there room for dialogue and disagreement about sex and sexuality?

you have or scenario you face. However, I commit to walking alongside you as we analyze three areas of messy truth that can be applied to almost any relationship or community setting. I hope you'll consider how these ideas could be implemented in your context. Who knows? You might be solidified on what *not* to do!

Hopefully, this book will be more helpful than harmful. Whatever your reasons for reading it, please keep an open mind. *Messy Truth* isn't just another book written by a straight white guy telling some Christians to be nice to their gay neighbors, lesbian cousins, or transgender coworkers. If you assume that my social privilege or theological view of sexuality compromises the validity of this book (even though I was raised by three gay parents within a large activist-oriented LGBTQ community), then consider this question:

Is there room for dialogue and disagreement about sex and sexuality?

Whereas the narrow-mindedness of some Christians devalues people, has society's views on sexuality become so closed-minded that diversity of thought isn't allowed? Are only certain people allowed to engage in discussions about sexuality? Should disagreements dictate how people treat each other? Is it harmful to disagree on aspects of sexuality? Might there be room in the discussion for people of every race, social standing, gender, and sexuality? Perhaps a diversity of thinking and experiences would help us dialogue better about sexuality. Personal experience definitely amplifies a voice, but a lack of experience doesn't eliminate anybody's voice.

Instead of worrying about whether you agree with my ideas, I'm obsessed with helping you develop the tenacity to be intentional about loving people as Jesus does. In lieu of being stuck in your office, hiding in the crevices of a book, dozing off during a webinar, scrolling through social-media feeds, or eavesdropping on coffeehouse conversations, let's shatter your routine so you can leverage whatever to reach whomever for Jesus. People find and follow Jesus better in community, not isolation. Messy truth is best experienced and understood with others.

I eagerly anticipate your next steps to foster a culture where messy truth is acknowledged and lived out. I pray you will help start or improve a community where people can ask questions about Jesus, have difficult conversations, encourage one another to grow, and carry each other's burdens while following Jesus together.

BACK IN THE CONFERENCE ROOM

Let's finish this chapter where we began: in the conference room. I eventually made some observations about the women who had approached the staff member:

- Each couple loved God and sought to understand him.
- The women felt as though they belonged at the church.
- Ordinary individuals in the church influenced them.
- The women trusted the church leaders.
- The women never stopped loving one another, but at some point their theology shifted.
- The couples were brave enough to ask the staff for help in discerning God's will.
- Neither couple was looking for a quick answer.

After spending time with the church's leaders, I was pleased with the intentionality of their thinking and the substance of their conversation with each other:

- The church leaders cared for both families.
- Each leader loved God and desired his counsel.
- Challenging questions were allowed.
- People weren't scolded for not having answers.
- No one was judged as they shared thoughts or asked further questions.
- There was healthy dialogue and consideration for each other.
- Having the discussion as a group made each of us sharper.

Building on the couples' relationships with other people in the church, the leaders chose to embrace messy truth together. Unified as a team, they graciously faced reality, prioritized God in their conversations, and worked to discover God's will for the families. The whole situation felt and looked messy, yet the circumstance was uniquely beautiful.

Are you ready to be part of a community where people like these women were given margin to pursue Jesus? Interested in knowing how you can help your church, small group, friends, and family welcome such stories? It depends on how far you are willing to go. If you're ready, let's begin talking about messy truth.

2

WHAT IS MESSY TRUTH?

If you get to know my friend Becket Cook, you will quickly learn he's not a morning person. Working long hours and late nights in the fashion industry will do that to you. When I first met Becket, we met for lunch at a West Hollywood café. It was there that he trusted me with his story.

Becket was raised in a Catholic household in the Dallas suburbs, and he remembers first being attracted to men at age ten. As a teenager, he visited his first gay bar and discovered community. "I felt like I was finally with people who understood me," he said. "We were all misfits in society, so I identified with them. I felt free! Anywhere else, I felt like I couldn't express this deep, dark secret."[1]

Eventually, Becket moved to Tinseltown. Because he first worked as an actor and then as a successful fashion set designer, he was a regular at award shows and celebrity parties. He felt he had to maintain a certain appearance (staying in shape, achieving social status, and so on) or lose standing in his community,[2] and his pace of life became exhausting.

Becket was attending an A-list party in Paris when he began

rethinking life. "This isn't it. This has sustained me for a long time, but this is not doing anything for me anymore. This is not the meaning of life."[3]

One day while in a coffee shop, he met some guys who were studying the Bible at a nearby table. Near the end of their conversation, they invited Becket to their church in Hollywood. He visited, but he didn't expect the sermon to challenge his perception of religion.[4] Learning that faith is all about a relationship with God, Becket followed Jesus. He decided that sexuality would not comprise any part of his main identity and committed to celibacy.

Becket is not only one of the kindest and most faithful people I know but also a stellar example of messy truth and how it fits within community.

THE PRIMARY GUIDEPOSTS OF MESSY TRUTH

I'm not sure where Becket would be today had the coffee-shop crew not engaged with him. If the people in the coffee shop or the church decided to treat him differently, I don't know if he would be making the impact he is today. Thankfully, those believers earned influence with him. They provided Becket the room to ask questions, follow Jesus, open up about his past, acknowledge his struggles, answer God's call, and continue to grow in Christ.

Any community that's healthy enough to embrace Becket (or any of us, for that matter) despite differences and disagreements isn't developed overnight. Rarely do meaningful relationships "accidentally" happen. Friendships may sometimes develop by chance, but healthy relationships are forged through intentionally loving people well.

Without intentionality, we'll surround ourselves with only those who agree with us. It takes little effort to exclude people and ideas that are contrary to our opinions and experiences. As a result, Christ-centered life change rarely occurs in relationships and communities where dialogue isn't allowed. It would serve us well to ask questions about how intentional we are about loving people:

- What does my lack of intentionality allow?
- Who does my lack of intentionality exclude?
- How did I feel when I was left out?
- Who has been left out? Who hasn't?

Intentional communities have arms outstretched to everyone. Even people, churches, and groups that believe God designed marriage to be between a man and woman can adopt and maintain this loving posture. And a loving posture is necessary because our disagreements can quickly divide us.

Disagreements about sex and relationships can easily be driven only by emotion instead of both emotion and logic. Similarly, unloving attitudes will always escalate these conversations into unhelpful debates and conflicts. Theological differences don't constitute a betrayal of relationships. Disagreements don't have to end dialogues or cancel relationships.

> Intentional communities have arms outstretched to everyone.

No one should be less loving or loved less because of differing beliefs regarding sexuality, marriage, intimacy, and relationships.

Jesus said the two greatest commandments for his followers

are to love God and people (see Matthew 22:36–40). Now, here comes the understatement of the decade: *loving people isn't easy.* If you think love is easy, read 1 Corinthians 13:4–8 and get back to me! Even though love is as much a truth of God as anything else, loving others is one of the most challenging mandates for Jesus followers. Love never abandons anyone. Love is intentional about walking with people and growing closer to God. Love thinks deeply about individuals, helps believers to love others well, makes it easier for people to belong to community, and engages in dialogue. Loving anyone is sacrificial.

Loving my enemies demands the death of my ego. Loving my neighbors requires me to step outside myself to relate with them. If I want to connect with others, I have to strengthen my faith and integrity so as to manage my emotions. There are times when I have to be the bearer or recipient of difficult conversations. Neither is fun. Loving people is extremely challenging. It can be exhausting at times and can even feel messy.

Truth feels messy when our convictions (beliefs about and love for God), compassion (value of and posture toward anyone), and conversations (life-giving and challenging interactions) collide. We embody messy truth by holding on to our *convictions,* being *compassionate* toward anyone, and proceeding with life-giving *conversations.* Consider the profound responsibility that's produced when these three words are bound together. All three words rely on prayer, understanding, wisdom, and Scripture, but each word has different "friends" they bring to the table. Conviction brings doctrinal beliefs, emotions, resolved and unresolved trauma, and life lessons. Compassion always includes emotional attachments, relationships, childhood upbringing, previous and current pains, painful lessons, theological understanding, empathy, dialogue, and sacrifice. Conversations are accompanied by courage, commitment, decisions made and yet to be made, self-discipline, focus, determination, and patience.

Truth feels messy when our convictions, compassion, and conversations collide.

Many of those words (with their responsibilities and baggage) make us feel uncomfortable! Just to reiterate: truth isn't messy, but it feels and looks messy when it intersects with our lives, beliefs, and relationships.

Conviction, compassion, and conversations—while not comprehensive—are guideposts for all believers who persevere in the tension between their beliefs and experiences. Christians who are unafraid of messy truth will have

- conviction about God's words
- compassion for anyone
- conversations with everyone

My convictions, compassion, and conversations can make all the difference between someone following Jesus or thinking worse of him. So, how do these messy-truth guideposts work in life?

Let's use an example that we all probably agree on: lying is bad! We should pay attention when God says not to lie (conviction), because lying damages relationships. When someone we care about lies, we should help them understand what's tempting them to lie and when they are most susceptible to lying (compassion). In light of these things, we must commit to telling the truth and encouraging honesty and holding each other accountable to being honest (conversations). Telling the truth is a daily discipline that is best strengthened and admonished in the midst of community.

Here's another "Thou shalt not" that most believers would hold to: dishonoring God's name is wrong. Our careless use of his name is not an accurate representation of his holiness (conviction). Misusing his name steals his due glory and lessens how people view him, which makes society worse. Honoring God's name is one of the ways we represent our Father well and communicate his values to our culture (compassion). Therefore, we help each other honor God's name regardless of the language or culture in our interaction with others (conversations). Understanding the importance of honoring God by how we refer to him happens best with other people (community).

Seems simple enough, right?

Not so fast. God says not to lie, but are there times when lying actually helps people? If I give in to the temptation of lying, is there forgiveness and restoration? If I accidentally lie, does God discipline me? What if I have been lied to? Isn't there the messy truth of forgiving others?

Just as God has forgiven us, he tells us to forgive people because our bitterness hurts others and doesn't imitate God. As a Jesus follower, I *must* forgive, even when I don't feel like it. Truth can feel messy, even with seemingly simple, obvious commands like "Do not lie." I still have to battle with deciding either to drift with my desires or to follow Jesus. This kind of nuance is very noticeable when it comes to sex. Let's begin to unpack the three guideposts of messy truth in regard to sex and sexuality.

CONVICTIONS ABOUT GOD'S WORDS

In my many years of being alive, I've noticed that the majority of us view people and events subjectively more than objectively. There are a few reasons for this, one being that we are suckers for our own opinion. After all, what do we think about and talk to ourselves about most? *Ourselves.* And researchers estimate that the average person makes more than thirty-five thousand conscious decisions each day.[5] That's a lot of work! As several researchers and authors have discussed, human brains develop routines, habits, and solutions so they can move on to the next decision.[6] Add sin to the mix of how our minds function and we have the perfect recipe for self-centeredness. No wonder we can find it problematic to grow closer to God, be empathetic, be bold with our words, consider objective data, and value character!

Sinful human selfishness explains not only divisions in society but also why God's truth can be challenging to profess. Our tendencies to make impulsive decisions with shallow rationale have only been amplified by a polarized society. It's almost effortless to assume the worst of anyone who disagrees with us. Along these lines, convictions about God's words never begin with evaluations of others, but with self-reflection about our own relationship with God.

Let's turn to Mark 7:18–23 as an example of messy truth. Jesus said,

> "Don't you see that nothing that enters a person from the outside can defile them? For it doesn't go into their heart but

into their stomach, and then out of the body." (In saying this, Jesus declared all foods clean.)

He went on: "What comes out of a person is what defiles them. For it is from within, out of a person's heart, that evil thoughts come—sexual immorality, theft, murder, adultery, greed, malice, deceit, lewdness, envy, slander, arrogance and folly. All these evils come from inside and defile a person."

Most people I know would applaud Jesus here. When we read those "evil" words, we envision some of the worst people imaginable. Yet, if we really think deeper about what Jesus said, all of us are guilty of what Jesus mentioned in this passage. To some degree or another, every single one of us has allowed most if not all of those sinful attributes to hijack our thoughts and decisions.

Jesus conveys that God's primary concern is not what someone eats, but what's brewing in that person's heart. The real problem is whatever shapes an individual's negative emotions, hurtful words, unhealthy choices, and selfish actions. It's interesting—and perhaps uncomfortable—that in the passage, Jesus mentions sexual immorality first.

Jesus warned against *porneia* (see Matthew 15:19; 19:9; Mark 7:21), which is an umbrella term for various acts of sexual immorality.[7] First-century Jewish listeners would have remembered the sexual sins listed in Leviticus 18 and 20 when they heard Jesus use this word (they perceived the word to include any type of sexual intimacy outside marriage between a man and woman).[8]

Yet in an attempt to resolve the tension felt between what Jesus says and what society allows, we might explain away or redefine his words. I mean, how well does society respond to someone who believes that sex should stay between a man and woman in marriage? Most want few, if any, restrictions on sex. To some people, sex is more subjective than objective. Whatever doesn't hurt others is affirmed. And still, a subjective view of sex and sexuality raises more questions and leaves many unanswered.

Perhaps a better question to ask ourselves might be, "How am I responding to Jesus's words?" The implications of what Jesus says about sex might even offend you. Specifically, in Mark 7:20–23, Jesus said that our thoughts and decisions about sex can be evil and defiling. Although his words might feel insulting, it could be that our discomfort is a chance for us to stop and reflect:

- What word made me feel uncomfortable?
- What memories, pictures, and thoughts surfaced?
- Am I holding opinions contrary to Jesus's words?
- Do I give my experiences and emotions the same authority as I give God's words?
- Are they placed on a higher level than Scripture?
- How can I best align myself with Jesus's words?

Just because we are convinced that something is true for us doesn't make it the truth. Our disagreement with what Jesus, Paul, or the other biblical authors wrote doesn't make their words any less true. Part of what makes truth feel so messy is that God's truth always runs countercultural to society's opinions and trends. Swimming upstream can be an exceedingly uncomfortable experience. It feels messy to differ with the majority opinion or latest trend on sex, sexuality, and relationships. It's natural to fear such disagreement, because the consequences of disagreement can be severe.

Nonetheless, embracing messy truth starts with the belief that

God's words—as correctly interpreted in their literary and historical contexts—have more authority than our experiences, emotions, and opinions. While our experiences and emotions are real and incredibly significant, we should always seek to first align with Scripture instead of the other way around. Recognizing that Scripture holds vastly more authority than our emotions and views can be troublesome (to say the least). Doing so requires that we sacrifice our sense of power and control.

Apologist Frank Turek maintained, "Suppressed truth has terrifying implications because power rather than reason is the currency of influence for those unwilling to follow the truth."[9] Could it be that in the final analysis, most of us just want control of our own lives? I don't believe that the average person struggling with God's words on various topics is some sort of James Bond villain or evil critic. All of us have struggled to align ourselves with God's words and will do so again. Regardless of what the struggle might be, I think our convictions about God's words rises or falls on whether or not we're ready to surrender our notion of power and the "life we deserve" back to Jesus.

> However painful the act of continual surrender might be, it's the appropriate response to an awesome God.

It's challenging to love God well if we regard him like a ventriloquist doll by reinterpreting his challenging words in palatable ways. Jesus said otherwise in Luke 9:23: "Whoever wants to be my disciple must deny themselves and take up their cross daily and follow me."

Following Jesus is the continual act of surrendering our perceived illusion of power to God. However painful the act of continual surrender might be, it's the appropriate response to an awesome God. Author Eve Tushnet, who is Catholic and celibate because of her theological convictions, reminds us, "God doesn't promise that He'll only ask you for the sacrifices you agree with and understand."[10] While she's absolutely correct, God does promise us that we'll never be alone. He gives us the gift of himself and each other.

God designed us for one another, and we desperately need each other! When we contemplate giving up control of our lives or an area of our lives, it can look miserable. Fears of loneliness and isolation can creep in, but God's answer is the church. There is no better place to grow in faith than in a *redemptive community.* Our conviction about God's words is necessary for us as we develop compassion for anyone we might encounter.

COMPASSION FOR ANYONE

Contrary to popular opinion, *God's truth* is not a synonym for *rules to keep.* It's proof of how much God loves people. And if he loves and has compassion for people, we should do the same, no matter who "they" are or how "they" came into our lives.

One afternoon, I was reading at a high-top table in the Los Angeles airport while waiting for my flight when a woman approached me. She sported disheveled hair and a lot of makeup.

"I'm going to plant myself here," she said, spilling her stuff all over my table.

Startled, I replied, "Sure."

"What book are you reading?" she asked. Before I could answer, she said, "Do you like *The Hobbit*?"

She pulled out a miniature leather-bound version of it from her purse.

"Absolutely," I replied. "Amazing author. I love J. R. R.—"

"Tolkien!" she interrupted. "He gets it! We all struggle."

"Yup! Some of his ideas came from his personal struggles, and some were inspired by stories in the Bible."

"The Bible?" she asked suspiciously. "I've read it seven times. I don't like it."

"Wow!" I exclaimed, not believing what she'd just said. "I've never read a book I don't like seven times."

"I like some parts," she clarified. "Ruth and Esther. They're cool. Maybe there's a 'god' out there somewhere. Not a creepy-old-man-looking god who isn't any fun!"

I considered defending God but figured this was a time to listen.

She scooted closer. "Wanna know about my job?"

"Sure . . ."

"I'm a porn star!" she said with a *gotcha*-type expression. "You probably recognize me."

"No, I don't," I answered.

"That's nice to hear," she responded. Pointing to a man a few tables from us who was staring at us, she said, "He knows who I am!"

He quickly turned his attention to his wife or girlfriend sitting next to him.

"And this guy at the table next to us," she said loud enough for him to hear. "He's definitely seen my movies!" He shot an awkward smile before glancing down at his phone.

Looking back at me and in a softer tone she asked, "How do you think God feels about my job?"

"God loves you no matter what," I replied.

For the first time since arriving at my table, she was silent. I then asked her, "Do you like your job?"

"Who wouldn't? Don't I look happy?" she asked sternly without a smile.

"Are you?" I asked.

Before she could answer, her flight was announced on the speaker. "Are you going to Las Vegas?" she asked. "We could talk on the flight!"

"Not headed to Vegas, but please take care of yourself."

She nodded and walked to her gate.

While this woman was memorable for several reasons, her comments about God stood out: *Maybe there's a "god" out there somewhere. Not a creepy-old-man-looking god who isn't any fun!*

Sadly, sex defined much of her identity. Her apparent animosity toward God indicated that she was probably somewhat familiar with what he said about sex and relationships. Perhaps she or someone she cared for had suffered bad experiences with Christians. Whatever her reason was for having negative feelings about God, my heart broke for her. Her unresolved pain propelled her to label his words as ridiculous and unreliable. To her, the Bible was irrelevant because it was just another rule book. Stabilizing our insecurities in self-centered ways makes God's words seem like harsh rules rather than loving guardrails.

In light of Mark 7:18–23 and other similar passages, living within God's guardrails might be one of the most compassionate decisions we can make for others and ourselves. When we choose to walk outside God's guidance—whether by making unhealthy decisions or refusing to love others—everyone gets hurt.

Think about inviting the LAX woman to an event at your church or a gathering of your Christian friends. How welcome would she be? How would your friends react if she said she was a porn star? Who would be more welcome in your community: a white-collar thief, a church member who has attended for years without serving or tithing, a legalistic know-it-all, the gossipy next-door neighbor, or a porn star?

Our compassion runs only as deep as what we struggle with ourselves. Too often our idea of compassion for "the least of these" (Matthew 5:19; 25:40, 45) applies to just a few of these. Although multiethnicity flourishes in some cities and towns, people still usually live near those who have similar beliefs and views. Communities tend to relate to only those who think and act like the majority in the community. People face rejection if they don't fit the mold or meet the standard, all of which is contrary to what the early church looked like. It was very multiethnic, multigenerational, and multisocioeconomic. If we want to mirror the first church, perhaps we should look to the compassion that Jesus and other New Testament leaders showed.

CONVERSATIONS WITH EVERYONE

Conversations can be *the worst*. Whether you're an introvert who craves alone time, an extrovert who feels overwhelmed because you want to have so many conversations, or someone who's running from *that talk* you need to have with *that person,* conversations have the potential to ruin a week.

Here are some challenging questions I receive on a regular basis:

- "What's the best way to talk to my son about homosexuality?"
- "What should I say to my daughter about her new girlfriend?"
- "How should I come out to my parents?"
- "When should I talk to my friend about what the Bible says regarding sex?"
- "How do I respond to this social-media discussion?"
- "How can I best apologize to my grandson for how I've treated him?"
- "I tried to talk to my parents about being transgender, but they didn't react well, so what else can I say to them?"

These questions are paramount. No matter how well you may have loved people or explained God's words, a poorly handled conversation has the potential to kill relationships and severely discourage people. It might be that you didn't pray fervently or adequately prepare for a conversation. Regardless of the reason, poorly handled conversations cost more than we think.

Spiritually healthy conversations can lead us to grow in our faith. They're a component of how we encourage one another. We don't follow Jesus by ourselves; it's a team effort. When we work on ourselves and engage in a community comprised of Jesus followers, we will be more likely to make Christ-centered decisions. Character is crafted in community.

Regardless of the message, Jesus kept his convictions, maintained compassion for anyone, and valued conversations with everyone. He spent the bulk of his time with messy students who probably wrestled with what he taught. Whether within a group of three, a group of twelve, or a group of seventy-two and more, Jesus's students began to see him for who he really is. Within a community, their devotion began to shift toward him.

With Jesus as our main focus, we're about to dive headfirst into processing the first messy-truth goal: *conviction about God's words*. We're going to address God's view of people, relational guardrails, and community with one another. Ideas will be discussed, such as human value, purpose, and identity. Many questions will be raised.

> We don't follow Jesus by ourselves; it's a team effort.

The next three chapters lay the foundation for not only the rest of the book but also for our relationships with other people. No matter what people may believe, what their relationships look like, or how they self-identify, people want to believe that they are loved and belong somewhere. We're all in this life together and need to move forward with one another as we follow Jesus.

Because we're all fallen humans, messy truth is best lived out within a spiritually healthy community. That's where my life was changed. I'm pretty certain Becket agrees that his was as well. If you haven't already, I'm sure you will find the same to be true about your life too!

PART 1

CONVICTION ABOUT GOD'S WORDS

WHAT'S THE VALUE OF ANYONE?

Luke was attracted to guys ever since he could remember. He was born in the Philippines and moved with his family to Southern California when he was young. In middle school, Luke felt different. While that is the case for most middle school students, Luke's feeling different transformed into depression when he was in high school. His GPA dropped to a 0.6, and his parents weren't sure what was going on. Deep down inside, Luke felt that his depression stemmed from a lack of honesty with himself and his family about his attraction to men.

As Luke was growing up, his family practiced Buddhism and Catholicism and then started to attend a nondenominational Christian church. This particular church had thousands of attendees and was well known in the community. For several months, he, his brother, and his parents attended church, but that was the extent of their involvement. Soon thereafter, Luke felt the longing to be more involved in the church. When he was in high school, he went on a men's retreat, where he came to terms with what he believed about Jesus. After he got home from the retreat, he made the decision to get baptized. He started attending the church's young-adult ministry and looked for places to serve.

The strength and momentum he felt from his faith gave him the courage to start coming out to people. Luke decided to come out not to announce that he was in or pursuing a relationship; rather, he wanted to share about this part of his life with his loved ones. He first came out to his parents. His mother took Luke's news well, while his father was less receptive. Actually, his mother took it so well that she unabashedly began telling his extended family that he was gay. Much to his chagrin, she offered to send his second and third cousins to him if they wanted help coming out of the closet.

Luke started spending more time with his friend Tom, who was also same-sex attracted, though they were never in a relationship. When Tom discovered that Luke was attending church, he started asking Luke questions like "Why are you going to church?" "Are you sure that's where you want to hang?" "Don't you know they hate people like us?"

"Because I enjoy the people there, and they love me," Luke answered.

Later, Tom confessed to Luke, "I wish I had Christian friends who loved me for who I am."

Luke hasn't been in a relationship and doesn't plan to be. He pursues his faith more passionately than most believers I know. Regarding his decision to keep attending church, he said that he does so because people there have treated him with compassion and integrity.

When I first came to faith, I believed that Christians should maintain orthodox beliefs while emulating the love that people in society seem to have for each other. Thankfully, I no longer believe what I did back then. People in society are *not* treated well. Society marginalizes individuals by labeling them, overvaluing popular opinion, demanding conformity to the latest trends, and thriving on outrage.

Within each of us is a gravitational pull toward self and sin that destroys us and others. Our unresolved insecurity seduces us into preferring ego over humility, selfishness rather than gratefulness, and pleasure instead of the common good. We're tempted to structure our lives to our benefit and adopt values that justify our decisions and agenda. All these temptations place the fight at the center of our identity.

While everyone has different roles or identities in their lives (mom, dad, sister, cousin, coach, boss, student), there is always an overarching identity that drives our values. It's the lens through which we view the world. If we aren't careful, investing in the wrong main identity will eventually send us into a tailspin. What we focus on matters. Actually, it isn't *what* we focus on; it's *whom* our focus should be devoted to.

IMAGE, LIKENESS, PURPOSE

Whether we differ from people who (mistakenly) enjoyed *The Last Jedi* or have the Oak Ridge Boys set as their ringtone, their worth isn't less than anyone else's. Even so, we're prone to drift toward those who agree with us and demonize all the rest. When we're tempted to devalue others, asking the following two questions might help to get us back on track:

1. Who created them?
2. Who died for them?

The first question addresses the purpose of an individual, which Genesis 1:26–28 answers:

> God said, "Let us make mankind in our image, in our likeness, so that they may rule over the fish in the sea and the birds in the sky, over the livestock and all the wild animals, and over all the creatures that move along the ground."
>
> So God created mankind in his own image,
>   in the image of God he created them;
>   male and female he created them.
>
> God blessed them and said to them, "Be fruitful and increase in number; fill the earth and subdue it. Rule over the fish in the sea and the birds in the sky and over every living creature that moves on the ground."

God *crafted* everyone in his image and likeness. The word *image* means "something *cut out*," like a statue carved out of stone or wood. Similarly, *likeness* refers to a sketch or representation of something or someone.[1] While *image* and *likeness* fit the poetic structure in Genesis 1, their significance runs deeper than literary style. Pairing the words together reveals a timeless truth:

image + *likeness* = how people uniquely resemble God

Physique, bank accounts, educational degrees, or training never establish an individual's purpose. Purpose comes from above.

Everyone has equal intrinsic value, as each person carries the Creator's image and likeness. This idea was a cornerstone for Dr. Martin Luther King Jr.'s civil rights ministry. God's image and likeness remains ingrained in each person—despite their sin and unbelief—which affords humanity a unique relationship with God.

WHY WE'RE CREATED IN GOD'S IMAGE AND LIKENESS

To differentiate humans from other creatures, God created people to be highly relational, moral, intelligent, empathetic, and spiritual. I believe these five attributes might describe some ways *how* humanity is made in God's image and likeness.

God's commands in Genesis 1:26 reveal *why* he crafted people in his image and likeness: "so that they may *rule*." In other words, God wanted humans to be his representatives on earth. Even though other creatures might display some of the five attributes, the ability to perceive God and spiritually connect with him is unique to humans. It was this spiritual attribute that afforded Adam and Eve a special relationship with God. If his image and likeness allow his representatives to spiritually connect with him, then we are God's representatives because we bear his image and likeness. Humanity rules by representing God well. One immediate application of this truth is that all of our decisions are spiritual. A person's resolve to enter an intimate relationship is spiritual in nature. Whether it's budgets, habits, attitudes, or parenting, we cannot divorce spiritual reality from decisions we make or actions we take.

For example, my mother's decision to be in a relationship with her partner, Vera, had spiritual undertones, as did the relationship itself. When I discussed sexuality and relationships with my mom and Vera, they proudly referred to themselves as *extremists*. Their religious pursuits went to the extreme at times. Their spiritual quest brought them to a Methodist church, a Zen Buddhist altar, a Wiccan coven, and a Quaker house. In so many ways, they saw spirituality as something they controlled instead of entrusting themselves to God. Spiritual realities clearly reside behind our personal choices.

Far from transactional, God's image and likeness emphasize how relational he wants to be with us. Even after humanity's fall, God's image and likeness remain in everyone so they can spiritually perceive him and recognize the need to have *a relationship with him as his children.* Just as loving parents yearn to be close to their children, so does God desire a relationship with each of us.

> We cannot divorce spiritual reality from decisions we make or actions we take.

Asking, "Who created them?" reminds us that a person's value and purpose is connected to who created them. People are worth more than their circumstances, relationship statuses, personal values, occupations, and prior choices might imply. Everyone bears God's image and likeness—even celebrities.

CAITLYN JENNER AND YOU

As you already know too well, sexuality is a complex subject. Why? Obviously, humanity's separation from God has complicated everything. Our personal feelings, experiences, relationships, beliefs, self-perceived roles, and social expectations have made sexuality a lightning-rod issue for century after century. Quite famously, the potential complexity of sexuality was seen in the Jenner-Kardashian family.

As an Olympic gold medalist, Bruce Jenner was once considered "the world's greatest athlete."[2] Besides having careers in movies, television, auto racing, and business, Jenner was married three times (the most recent and notable wife being Kris Jenner, the mother of the Kardashian daughters). In April 2015, Jenner came out to the world as a trans woman.

On June 1, 2015, Jenner was featured as Caitlyn Jenner on the cover of *Vanity Fair*.[3] People on social media joined bloggers, journalists, celebrities, and news commentators to praise Jenner's bravery. Additionally, Jenner had more than a few critics—and the most influential critics weren't religious conservatives.

During one interview, Diane Sawyer asked if Jenner celebrated President Barack Obama's mention of transgender people in his 2015 State of the Union address. Jenner's response surprised many and drew multiple criticisms:

"Not to get political, I've just never been a big fan. I'm kind of more on the conservative side."

"Are you Republican?" Sawyer asked.

"Yeah," he said with a smile. "Is that a bad thing? I believe in the Constitution."[4]

In 2016, Jenner supported President Donald Trump's presidential bid. In an interview that year, Jenner said, "It was easy to come out as trans. It was hard to come out as Republican."[5]

In the upcoming months, attacks on Jenner weren't limited to politics. Actress Rose McGowan chided Jenner:

> You do not understand what being a woman is about at all. . . .
> We are more than deciding what to wear. We are more than the stereotypes foisted upon us by people like you. . . . We have had a VERY different experience than your life of male privilege.[6]

In September 2015, Jenner appeared on *The Ellen DeGeneres Show* claiming to be a traditionalist who hadn't always been supportive of marriage equality but was so now.[7] Later, DeGeneres was on *The Howard Stern Show,* where she claimed that Jenner seemed to have "judgment about gay people and marriage."[8] Needless to say, the already lively chatter surrounding Jenner intensified.

In a matter of months, Jenner came out as a trans woman, resonated with being asexual,[9] appeared at the Republican National Convention, and purported to be somewhat of a traditionalist who supported gay marriage. People were frustrated because Jenner didn't align with society's expectations of whom trans women should vote for or what they should believe (notice our propensity to categorize each other?). Jenner's experiences highlighted the emotionally charged complexity that surrounds sexuality, but more specifically identity.

One popular dictionary defines *identity* as "the fact of being who or what a person or thing is,"[10] while another dictionary designates it as "the distinguishing character or personality of an individual."[11] Our identity communicates our uniqueness, passions, and values. It's the lens through which we interpret life. It could be argued that we have multiple identities to embrace or roles to step into. I'm a husband, father, son, family member, friend, pastor, author, Star Wars geek . . . You get the picture.

Humanity has been in an identity crisis ever since sin entered the world. It's a crisis that everyone faces. This crisis can easily distort answers to questions like:

- Who am I?
- Why do I exist?
- What should I do with my life?
- Who do I relate to the most?

Coming to terms with *who you are* can be a long and strenuous task. If we aren't careful, we could view our attributes, achievements, relationships, and occupations as the most significant aspects of our ultimate identities. We might even primarily identify with a failure or begin to believe that we actually *are* our mistakes.

Christian psychologists Dr. Mark Yarhouse and Dr. Lori Burkett wisely advise their readers and clients, "Expand your focus so you are not overly consumed with your sexual orientation at the expense of the many other dimensions of your sexual identity and sense of yourself as a person."[12]

Though your sexuality (birth sex, gender, and so on) is incredibly meaningful, it can't sustain the weight of your primary identity. God never designed sexuality to represent the totality of who you are or to be your essential defining aspect. Actually, nowhere in the Bible do we see any leader base their main identity on any aspect of their sexuality. Even so, we keep searching for an identity that grants us the illusion of control.

We humans are experts at constructing negative thought patterns, unhealthy habits, and blame in order to keep our insecurities at bay. Sooner or later, our insecurities and flaws *will* break free. One day our unresolved past will show up again like an uninvited second cousin at a family reunion! We cannot protect ourselves from ourselves by ourselves. Each of us needs a redemptive community because our insecurities always catch up with us. I believe God allows us to face consequences and endure pivotal circumstances for many reasons (not the least of which is for us to have another opportunity to surrender to him).

When we forget our or someone else's ultimate identity, we need to ask the second question from page 44: "Who died for them?"

WHO DIED FOR THEM?

Satan tempted Eve in Genesis 3:5: "God knows that when you eat from it your eyes will be opened, and you will be like God, knowing good and evil."

Notice what Satan attacked first: her identity. He promised, "You will be like God." He basically said, *You don't need God. Take control over your life. You decide what's good and evil.*

Sound familiar? The creature longed to usurp the Creator.[13] It wasn't enough for Adam and Eve to bear God's image and likeness; they wanted to be God. Satan lured them into repeating his heavenly rebellion.

Immediately after rebelling, Adam and Eve's relationship with God was severely damaged. Their spiritual connection with him was busted. The harmonious relationship they enjoyed with other creatures was wrecked. Their moral compasses began spinning out of control, and their ability to perfectly understand each other was turned upside down. Even today, the world still feels the consequences of their decision, as Paul laments in Romans 8:20–22.

More than disobedience, Adam and Eve's sin was an ugly coup that recycles itself in our daily lives. Every sin that you and I commit is an attempt to take the spotlight away from God and shine it on ourselves. As much as we carry God's image and likeness, we also live with and in the consequences of sin. Yes, we are saved and God has taken up residence in us, but we also live with the reality that we are sinners. Let me take it a step further: we are capable of almost any sin.

Thankfully, God is abundantly gracious and patient with us. He never gives up on his children. *Never.* In Genesis 3:15, as God addresses the serpent, he made this promise to Adam and Eve:

> I will put enmity
>> between you and the woman,
>> and between your offspring and hers;
> he will crush your head,
>> and you will strike his heel.

Through Jesus, God fought to reconcile his relationship with his rebellious representatives—and he's still fighting for us. Jesus is the answer to the question "Who died for them?"

Hebrews 1:3 might be one of the clearest expressions of this truth: "The Son is the radiance of God's glory and the *exact repre-*

sentation of his being, sustaining all things by his powerful word." Humans might *resemble* God because they bear his image, but Jesus is the *exact* representation of God. And when we follow Jesus, we immediately start growing to be like him.

In the New Testament, Paul wrote the most about this truth. I appreciate how the NLT translates his words in Romans 8:3, "He sent his own Son in a body like the bodies we sinners have. And in that body God declared an end to sin's control over us by giving his Son as a sacrifice for our sins." In Romans 8:29 and 1 Corinthians 15:49, Paul taught that Christians will be conformed into Jesus's image and "are being transformed into his image with ever-increasing glory, which comes from the Lord, who is the Spirit" (2 Corinthians 3:18). He encouraged the believers in Colossae to "put on the new self, which is being renewed in knowledge in the image of its Creator" (Colossians 3:10).

Jesus, God's exact representation and perfect representative, reestablished our relationship through the Cross and Resurrection. As a result, Jesus *must* be preeminent in a Christian's life.

Our Relationship with Jesus Should Be
Our Primary Identity

Jesus should be our primary identity—nothing more, nothing less. He is *the* example of what identifying with God looks like. He's the poster child for someone who completely identifies with God.

If you follow Jesus, identifying with him was the last decision you ever made. All of the following decisions in your life belong to God. When you chose to follow Jesus, you died. In a sense, when Jesus died, God saw *you* on that cross. God counted you as dead at Golgotha with Jesus (see Romans 6:8, Colossians 2:20,

2 Timothy 2:11, and Revelation 14:13). Dead people don't fight for control over their lives because, well, they're dead!

Although God saw you on the cross, he now sees Jesus living through you. Christ should be your *very* life. Paul said as much in Colossians 3:3, "You died, and your life is now hidden with Christ in God," but then in verse 4 he qualified our relationship with Jesus in a unique way: "When Christ, *who is your life,* appears, then you also will appear with him in glory."

Paul also described this same idea in Galatians 2:20: "I have been crucified with Christ and I no longer live, but Christ lives in me." Many other passages—such as Romans 8:10, 2 Corinthians 13:5, Ephesians 3:17, Philippians 1:21, and 1 John 5:11–12—teach Christ's ownership of his followers' lives. Because Jesus, the perfect representation, died and rose for humanity to God's glory, he should define and be the main identity for each of his followers. Whose you are determines who you are. Jesus owns whomever he redeems.

> Whose you are determines who you are.

There are few who are as passionate about redemption and identity in Christ as Greg Johnson. He's attracted to men but is single because of his biblical beliefs. As he was growing up, he described himself as an atheist who tried to conceal his sexual orientation. Greg became a Christian when he was in college. After graduating, he enrolled in seminary and is currently the lead pastor at Memorial Presbyterian Church in St. Louis, Missouri.

When describing his identity in Christ, Greg says:

The gospel doesn't erase this part of my story so much as it redeems it. My sexual orientation doesn't define me. It's not the most important or most interesting thing about me. It is the backdrop for that, the backdrop for the story of Jesus.[14]

Greg exemplifies the consistent surrender of our lives back over to Jesus so we can live by faith. He's living out what Paul wrote in the second half of Galatians 2:20: "The life I now live in the body, I live by faith in the Son of God, who loved me and gave himself for me."

Not only has Jesus brought us into God's family, but our goal in life is to identify with him so we can be just like him. Identifying primarily with Jesus means

- we love him above all else
- we appreciate grace
- we tell others about him
- we serve his bride, the church
- we base our values off God's words
- we live in relationships as he and other New Testament authors described

Looking at the whole perspective, God created humans in his image and likeness so we could represent him. And he sent his Son, Jesus, to pay the debt incurred by the betrayal (sin) of his image bearers. Because of these two things, whomever God created and Jesus died for has equal intrinsic value.

> Jesus redeems the flaws and bad moments in your story.

Your personal value stems from who created you and who died for you, not what you've achieved or haven't accomplished. Jesus redeems the flaws and bad moments in your story. Your regrets, unhealthy habits, toxic relationships, lack of humility, negative feelings about yourself, or _____ (fill in the blank) are not the primary aspects of your identity.

Understanding who you are is vital to grasping messy truth, because how you view yourself determines how you'll treat others.

LATE NIGHT WITHOUT MEDICATION

Sitting in their living room, I cried with two women I had met just hours earlier. At the time, I was consulting with a large church where these two women were attending. When they first started attending there, it didn't take them long to figure out that the church did not affirm same-sex relationships. Even so, they kept attending because the people in the church treated them like royalty.

After attending the church for a year, the women came to the conclusion that God created marriage to be between a man and woman. Similar to the couples in the first chapter, they approached a church leader and asked about their next steps. Now I was in the couple's living room processing their situation.

The women, Tamara and Shanice, had been in a relationship for ten years and married the past three of those years. They told me that even though their own study led them to the decision to divorce, there were significant obstacles in their path.

"I can imagine," I replied, unintentionally and erroneously rushing past their lament.

Almost staring me down, Tamara firmly said, "No, I don't think you can."

Quickly realizing my ignorance, I said, "I'm sorry. Please tell me more."

They told me that love for each other was a difficult obstacle. Shanice, who appeared frail, was disabled. According to her, sexual intimacy was impossible. However, the seemingly overwhelming barrier was that if they divorced, Shanice would lose her health insurance.

"She has schizophrenia," Tamara stated. "You know she needs her medication!"

"I just about got shot the last time I didn't have it," Shanice said as she stared at the floor.

"Can you tell me what happened?" I asked.

"I could've sworn I heard my niece and nephew yelling at me from outside my door," Shanice began, pointing at the front door of the apartment we were in. "So I called to them from just outside my door. Then I walked down to the street and yelled louder so they'd hear me. Before I knew it, the police were there. They started telling me to do something, but I . . . I couldn't understand what they were saying," she related as if she were reliving the moment.

"I heard the officers' voices and the voices of what I thought was my family at the same time. I couldn't tell the difference . . . couldn't tell them apart."

Shanice paused and looked at Tamara, who gently squeezed her hand.

"I . . ." Shanice began and her voice cracked. "One cop took out her gun and pointed it at me." Silence filled the apartment as the emotion set in.

"I . . . I dropped to the ground."

More silence. Tamara's eyes were welling with tears. So were mine.

"I understand why they didn't know what was going on," Shanice continued. "It's not easy being a black schizophrenic lesbian without medication when it's late at night and the police assume you've lost it."

"Does God want her to be in physical danger?" Tamara asked.

Pulling it together, I answered, "I don't make a habit of speaking for God, but my answer would be no. You have a church that loves you and is willing to walk with you. I think God uses community to provide for us in more ways than we know."

I suggested they go back to their church leaders and ask them to walk with them during this season. After we talked about options regarding their circumstance, I left their apartment.

Over the years, I've had one too many encounters with churches that falsely advertise everyone is welcome. Their treatment of people shows they don't really welcome everyone. And by "welcome," I don't mean that church leaders need to be in agreement with a person's relationship decisions. Rather, welcome means fostering a community in which anyone feels and believes they could be part of that particular community and that, regardless of their past or present, they are treated with dignity because of who created them and who died for them. Tamara and Shanice had found such a community where they were seen as part of *everyone* rather than treated like just *anyone*.

EVERYONES AND ANYONES IN COMMUNITY

You and I have our "everyones" and "anyones." People you place in the "everyone" category are individuals you basically have no problem with. Sure, you disagree here and there, but when push comes to shove, you feel good about them, speak well of them, and treat them with respect.

Those you put in the "anyone" category are individuals you have significant differences with. They might have different political beliefs, work for organizations you cannot stand, or are in relationships you can't understand. Usually, the way you feel about your anyones is revealed by your words, actions, and posture toward them. Left to ourselves, we can begin treating almost everyone like an anyone. When in a spiritually healthy and redemptive community, we have accountability and encouragement to value people because of who created them and who died for them.

Tamara and Shanice encountered Christians in their church who treated them like everyones. In other words, their value was affirmed. People in the church saw them as women whom God created and Jesus died for. The relationships they had formed in the church began to inspire them to place their identity in Christ. Just as their church friends were already walking with these women,

> Community helps people discover and strengthen their identity in Jesus.

they were willing to continue journeying with the women as they prepared to make a difficult decision. Community made a difference in the lives of these women.

Community helps people discover and strengthen their identity in Jesus. Community provides chances for people to ask questions about God, dialogue about disagreements, discover who they are, process life, and continually learn how to love others well. In other words, a community that embraces messy truth is filled with relationships that are redemptive in nature. Studies have proven that the rates of suicides and attempted suicides of transgender individuals drops significantly when they feel supported by a redemptive community.[15] Feeling valued matters.

WILL YOU TRUST WHAT JESUS SAYS EVEN WHEN YOU DISAGREE WITH HIM?

Many of these students don't see why sex is such a big deal." That's what Jeremy said a few moments before I was about to speak at a student winter retreat. Jeremy served as a youth pastor at a large church in Southern California. Every winter, he and the youth staff would take their middle school and high school students to the mountains for a retreat. Several years ago, he had invited me to be the main speaker.

"What?" I yelled. Even though we were standing at the back of the auditorium, I was having difficulty hearing him as a couple hundred students were singing songs to God.

He motioned for me to follow him outside. We were met with extremely cold air and a snowfall that was growing more and more intense. Our coats did little to protect us from the sudden arctic temperatures of the Southern California mountains.

"I couldn't hear you," I explained.

"Caleb, I should've told you this, but most of these students don't understand what the big deal is with sex. Most of them probably disagree with what the Bible teaches about it."

"I get that," I answered.

"So you can't preach in the traditional way with a 'Thus saith the Lord' attitude," he went on, trying to coach me.

"Jeremy," I said as my teeth chattered, "I have two things to say. First, I don't preach like that, but I appreciate the encouragement. Second, it's cold. Can we please go back inside and then you can evaluate my message when I'm done?"

He laughed and gave me a reassuring pat on the back as we walked back into the retreat auditorium.

Okay, truth be told, I hadn't considered that some or all the students may not agree with what God had to say about sex. I acted as if I had because I wanted to get out of the cold weather but also because I wanted to save face. Soon I was back inside the warm auditorium with the band playing the second-to-last song. Almost time to go and preach!

Come on, Caleb! I thought. *You already knew that about students, so why didn't you think about it?*

I began to sweat from the nervousness I was feeling. It was too late to rewrite the sermon, so maybe I could reorder the outline? Focusing on the sermon in that moment was tough because my heart was breaking for those students.

Too many students and adults have bought into the lie that integrity, sex, and morals are almost completely subjective. In one way or another, the idea that "what we feel is more important than what we know" resounds from almost every public platform. We will always be competing against God for control of our lives when our emotions primarily determine our decisions. Is there little doubt as to why society interprets Christian ethics, values, and ideas to be anti-intellectual and at times even harmful? So, how can we help people value logic in a society that overemphasizes emotions and reactions?

I don't know about you, but I can't remember the last time I made a really good, impulsive, emotionally reactive decision. Sooner or later, we'll find ourselves to be lost if our feelings primarily lead our life's journey. It's vital for our logical minds and our emotions to work together as we embrace messy truth and build a community that helps people find and follow Jesus. As we head into this chapter, please read and process with both authentic feelings and critical thinking.

TRYING TO TRAP JESUS

One day the Pharisees attempted to trap Jesus with a question. Because they valued power more than they did people, the Pharisees asked if a man could divorce his wife for any reason. Though numerous rabbinical teachings on marriage had clouded clarity on divorce, Jesus's reply in Matthew 19:4–6 was nothing short of brilliant:

> "Haven't you read," he replied, "that at the beginning the Creator 'made them male and female,' and said, 'For this reason a man will leave his father and mother and be united to his wife, and the two will become one flesh'? So they are no longer two, but one flesh. Therefore what God has joined together, let no one separate."

While there are many opinions on how to interpret Genesis 1–3, those verses still reflect the early Israelites' understanding of humanity's origin, God's image, individual purpose, the male and female relationship, and the design of sexual intimacy (Jesus invoked the authority of Genesis 1–2). Regardless of our personal opinions, Jesus's words about the matter are priceless.

> Marriage is first and foremost God's covenant, not ours. He takes responsibility for the relationships in the covenant he created.

Not even mentioning rabbinical teaching on marriage, Jesus's response in Matthew 19:4–6 stood on Scripture alone. By referring to Genesis 1:27 and 2:24 in his response to the Pharisees, Jesus would have caused them to recall the surrounding verses.[1] Genesis 1:26–28 and 2:20–24 are filled with words and metaphors that describe marriage. Even the Hebrew words for "man" and "woman" in Genesis 2:23–24 can be translated *husband* and *wife*.[2] The words depicting the son's departure from his parents and joining to his wife (*leaves* and *is united*) are used elsewhere in the Old Testament to describe covenants.[3] Jesus redirected his listeners' attention to what's really at stake: the marriage covenant.

If God created humanity in his own image, purposed the male/female relationship to be in a covenant relationship with him, and placed sexual intimacy within the covenant relationship, then he owns it all—everything and everyone involved. Marriage is first and foremost God's covenant, not ours. He takes responsibility for the relationships in the covenant he created.

THE MARRIAGE COVENANT SHOULD BE UNBREAKABLE

The Pharisees tried to discredit Jesus with a second question, but his answer in Matthew 19:7–9 is brilliant:

"Why then," they asked, "did Moses command that a man give his wife a certificate of divorce and send her away?"

Jesus replied, "Moses permitted you to divorce your wives because your hearts were hard. But it was not this way from the beginning. I tell you that anyone who divorces his wife, except for sexual immorality, and marries another woman commits adultery."

Few seriously consider the implications of Jesus's narrow view of divorce.[4] His words about divorce are just as unpopular now as back then. Jesus's countercultural views are probably one of many reasons that people cling to a fake image of Jesus—one who agrees with all their political views, opinions about others, and choices of relationships. Unapologetically, Jesus was always countercultural to both the religious and secular communities. More times than not, Jesus had to inspire people to think the opposite of what they were thinking.

The Pharisees' original question to Jesus was about divorce, but Jesus redirected their focus to the marriage covenant. Truly, the arrogance of the Pharisees is astounding. Think of it this way—the Pharisees wanted to debate the rights they had as humans over a covenant that God created and owns. God's covenant mattered more to Jesus than to the Pharisees.

Jesus had a narrow view of marriage not only because God created the marriage covenant but because the covenant includes God. He honors and defends God in the circumstances which involve him. For instance, Jesus was angry when the temple was turned into a strip mall. The money changers took advantage of the place where God received worship. Jesus's view of God was supremely higher than his religious counterparts.

Still, there are those who believe that Jesus could have held a more progressive view of marriage than what we know. However, that doesn't align with his words about marriage. If Jesus had a literal interpretation of Genesis 1:27 and 2:24, why would he relax his interpretation for marriage? If he had a narrow view of divorce, what sense does it make for him to have an open view of marriage?

MARRIAGE IS SYMBOLIC OF A GREATER RELATIONSHIP

Jesus wasn't the only New Testament figure to quote Genesis 2:24. Paul believed that sex and marriage were spiritually bound together. Among his other warnings against sexual immorality in 1 Corinthians, Paul quoted Genesis 2:24 in 1 Corinthians 6:16 as he warned believers against having sex with prostitutes.[5] In Ephesians 5:21–33, Paul illustrated ways in which husbands and wives should submit to one another. In verses 31–32, he concluded, " 'For this reason a man will leave his father and mother and be united to his wife, and the two will become one flesh.' This is a profound mystery—but I am talking about Christ and the church."

God seems to use Adam and Eve, as well as every marriage since, to foreshadow the ultimate marriage between Jesus and the church.[6] Much in these verses (Genesis 1:27; 2:24; Matthew 19:4–9) lines up with Jesus's strong opposition of sexual immorality. Thus, Jesus's reference to Genesis 1:27 and 2:24 is more than an answer to his detractors; it's his belief about marriage:

- Jesus's appeal to Genesis 1:27 as God's creation of humans with distinct genders

- In Genesis 2:23–24, the Hebrew words for *man* and *woman* can also be translated as "husband" and "wife"
- Hebrew words in Genesis 2:24 being used elsewhere in the Old Testament to describe covenants
- Picture of parents in Genesis 2:24
- Illustration of the new marriage between the son and his wife in Genesis 2:24
- Jesus's use of Genesis 1:27 and 2:24 as an answer to marriage
- Jesus's pronouncement of "what God has joined together" in Mark 10:8–9

Given Jesus's words about marriage and sex, I believe:

God designed sexual intimacy for marriage between a man and a woman.

Sexual intimacy is a unique and private expression of love intended for the marriage covenant. God designed it to reflect his unconditional love. It's supposed to be one of the most transparent and honest expressions of intimacy between a husband and wife . . . but, just as with everything else, we want to take ownership of what we never created.

OBJECTIONS

Theologian and Baptist minister William Webb wrote *Slaves, Women, and Homosexuals,* in which he investigated Scripture passages referring to homosexuality, slavery, and women. Webb argued that when reading the Bible, we must differentiate between cultural (applied to a context) and transcultural (applied to everyone) passages to see if there's a progression or plateau of these topics.[7] His research shows issues of slavery and women to be cultural because there's progression away from "tradition" (not to mention the strong argument to be made that God is not pro-slavery). Webb also found no progression toward the affirmation of intimate relationships outside marriage between a man and woman; thus, those verses are transcultural.

Though various types of marriages are portrayed in Scripture and present in other cultures surrounding Israel, it's misleading to assume those relationships were equally affirmed by God. I appreciate what New Testament scholar Darrell Bock says: "Show me a text in the Bible where this area is handled neutrally or positively. Just name me one."[8] Nowhere in Scripture does any rabbi affirm relationships outside marriage between a man and woman. "Never once do we see a Jewish leader, thinker, writer, or rabbi sanction any form of same-sex erotic behavior. They condemned pederasty, same-sex peer relations (both male and female), and even same-sex marriages, although the latter were rare in those days—rare but not nonexistent as some have argued."[9] In my opinion, the male/female relationship launched in Genesis 1:26–28 is woven through the Bible.

Aren't Monogamous Same-Sex Relationships New?

In one of his many interviews, renowned scholar N. T. Wright alluded that monogamous same-sex relationships existed even before the first century:

As a classicist, I have to say that when I read Plato's *Sympo-sium,* or when I read the accounts from the early Roman em-pire of the practice of homosexuality, then it seems to me they knew just as much about it as we do. . . . This is not a modern invention, it's already there in Plato. The idea that in Paul's today it was always a matter of exploitation of younger men by older men or whatever . . . of course there was plenty of that then, as there is today, but it was by no means the only thing.[10]

Despite evidence pointing to monogamous same-sex relation-ships in the first century, some scholars insinuate that Jesus and the New Testament authors had no concept of monogamous same-sex relationships.[11] Now, I agree the modern idea of same-sex marriage was nowhere to be found in the first century Roman society.[12] However, I find it difficult to believe that there was no form of monogamous same-sex relationships. Here's a deep thought—humans have always been humans. It's extremely plau-sible to believe such relationships existed in Paul's day. If this is probable, then it's ridiculous to assume Paul and other New Tes-tament leaders were clueless about such relationships.

Keep a few things in mind when considering Paul's probable knowledge of monogamous same-sex relationships. We're talking about the same man who regularly studied a variety of topics (Scripture, tradition, culture, and so on). As a Pharisee, he was an expert in theology and tradition. Being a Roman citizen, he un-derstood Roman law. Paul could go toe to toe with Athenian phi-losophers and engage Jewish scholars all in the same day while still having time for dinner. He even desired to go to Spain.

Yet despite Paul's exhaustive knowledge of theology and culture in the first century, when he wrote about marriage and sex, he didn't include exceptions for monogamous same-sex relationships (he doesn't even mention them). Is that a problem? Not really. Should we make a list of first-century people, causes, events, and writings that New Testament authors barely mentioned or did not at all? Roman politics, pagan deities, and historical events are among the many examples of what is not or is hardly found in the New Testament, but they existed. I believe the same is true of monogamous same-sex relationships.

CONVICTIONS DON'T COMPROMISE A PERSON'S VALUE

Why am I talking so much about what Jesus said and so little about what other biblical leaders wrote about sex, marriage, and so on? People who do not attend church or identify as Christian still usually respect or admire Jesus. If people find Jesus to be likable, then Jesus is a starting point to relate with them. And Jesus didn't just like people; *he valued them.*

He taught that men and women possess equal value (which was taboo in the first century). Besides honoring marriage because God created it, Matthew 5:32 shows he valued women enough to stand up for their marriages: "I tell you that anyone who divorces his wife, except for sexual immorality, makes her the victim of adultery, and anyone who marries a divorced woman commits adultery." Rabbinical teachings based on faulty interpretations of Scripture allowed Jewish men to divorce their wives for nearly any reason. What do you think happened to women who had been divorced in a male-dominated first-century Middle

Eastern society? With few ways to earn money, they either remarried or faced a bleak future. But Jesus valued women who were divorced. He saw worth in women who were sick, stood by wells, were caught in adultery, and even washed his feet. He had female followers. Jesus interacted with Roman centurions and other individuals who probably committed sexual immorality (if even only in their thoughts).

He also said things no one else said: "Love your enemies and pray for those who persecute you. . . . Love your neighbor as yourself. . . . Love your enemies, [and] do good to those who hate you. . . . Love one another. As I have loved you, so you must love one another. . . . As the Father has loved me, so have I loved you" (Matthew 5:44; 22:39; Luke 6:27; John 13:34; 15:9).

> Loving and valuing others despite disagreements earns influence.

In John 15:12, he challenged his followers to do the same: "My command is this: Love each other as I have loved you."

Loving people can be costly, but refusing to love costs even more! In my life, I tend to trust those who make me feel loved and valued more than I trust those who do not. People who have invested in me without condemning me have greater influence in my life than they probably realize. Loving and valuing others despite disagreements earns influence.

My friend Barry Corey is the president of Biola University and an example of this principle. In his book *Love Kindness,* Barry described spending a year as a researcher in Southeast Asia and befriending Karen, who is a lesbian. Karen talked with him about another woman she was in a relationship with. Barry asked her why she chose to discuss that topic with him. He said,

She wasn't asking me to consider changing my position or becoming an advocate. . . . But she told me because she knew if I was living out my faith as a Christian, I'd receive her with grace first, not judgment. She trusted I wouldn't backpedal on my confession that if I love God, I also must love my neighbor as myself.[13]

It's acceptable to disagree on theological ideas, but it's always wrong to dehumanize others—even when they disagree with you. The more that people feel valued by you, the more they feel as though they could get to know others like you. It's the beginning of fostering the kind of redemptive community that inspires people to follow Jesus no matter the cost.

TRUSTING JESUS WHEN WE DISAGREE

Going back to my story from the beginning of the chapter, I was nervous as I got up onstage to speak to the students. I hadn't changed my content, but I did shift my approach. I talked about a couple of friends who had difficult experiences in relation to their sexuality. Then I told the students that even if they didn't go to church, they probably knew the Bible had seemingly strict guardrails concerning sex. Then I asked, "Why does God want sex to stay in a marriage between a man and a woman if he knew people would be attracted to people of the same sex?"

Complete silence.

"Here's my best theological answer," I began. "I don't know."

More silence . . . so I continued.

"But we can't just brush off God's words by saying, 'The Bible doesn't address that question, so we need to use our best logic.' The biblical authors were silent on many issues, but their silence doesn't allow us to do whatever we want. There's a larger biblical idea at the root of every unaddressed circumstance in the Bible that can guide our thinking. Along this line of thought, even though Jesus never mentioned same-sex relationships, he did talk about sex outside marriage."

Not to sound harsh, but I don't need to know *why* God says something. I'm not proposing that it's wrong to ask God "why" questions. I don't want to dismiss those who want to know why. I get how the why is important (especially in light of attraction, emotions, faith, pain, and so on). God invites us to dialogue with him. But whether we want to admit it or not, getting an answer to our *why* questions isn't necessary for our dialogue with God or devotion to him.

We should try our best not to let "why" become an obstacle to growing our relationship with God. If we truly believe he is all powerful and in control, then we'd also agree that God has looked down the corridors of time and seen things that we have not. Maybe God sees the fallout of our brokenness and how people underestimate the power of sex. I mean, sex is so powerful that it doesn't even have to be an action to hurt us. Sex, inappropriately manifested in our thoughts, damages us (see Matthew 5:27–30). Sex can dramatically alter our emotions, decisions, behavior, physical health, personal confidence, finances, friendships, and occupation. It has influenced politics, social media, movies, songs, and books.

Ironically enough, no one ever died because of a lack of sex, but plenty of individuals have died because of sex. Even more have been hurt because of sex. We (especially men) have a propensity to use sex to establish and maintain power. Doing so will always harm others. Lying about, exaggerating, or gossiping about sexual escapades has wrecked people and families. Regardless of what it looks like, fulfilling selfish desires at someone else's expense destroys lives and makes society worse.

Are you willing to trust Jesus even though you may not agree with him? Are you willing to keep trusting Jesus even if you die with more unanswered questions than answered ones? Even though God doesn't answer all our questions or explain all his reasoning, he always offers us invitations to trust him. And though it might not feel like it in the moment, trusting Jesus always works out for the best.

WHEN DOES BELONGING HAPPEN?

A few years ago, I was consulting with a church on the East Coast. I reached out to a college friend in the area to get together and catch up. He recommended we meet at the church where I was consulting, as they had a coffeehouse where we could sit and chat. Soon after arriving in the city, I made my way to the church. I love to visit different churches and observe their culture—their hospitality, beliefs, design and architecture, the attitudes of those in the actual church building, and so on. Walking into the lobby, I immediately noticed three words in big letters plastered on the wall for everyone to see. The words were stacked on top of each other with arrows in between to show the progression. They were:

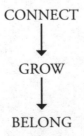

CONNECT

GROW

BELONG

I immediately wondered why the word *belong* was last in the list.

Maybe it's a good thing they have *connect* as the first word. Who knows? But I wasn't so sure that I liked the order of the words. It could be that I'm being picky, but I don't think so. As I stared at the words, other questions began to fill my head:

- Do these words correspond to a relationship with the church or with God?
- Does the church connect with people first, or do people connect with the church first?
- Shouldn't there be a fourth or fifth word? (That's the preacher side of me.)

Back home in Southern California, I shared my frustration regarding the scenario with a friend who's a pastor. He smiled and asked me a question that frustrated me even more. However, the more I processed his question, the more I felt resolve to my frustration. Then a few days later, his question began to frustrate me more. (By the way, really good questions are like roller coasters: they take you on loops and can plunge in directions you weren't expecting.) Here was his question: *Does belonging precede life change, or do we belong because our lives changed?*

In other words, does a relationship with Jesus grant me a place in a specific local church, or should local churches create spaces for people to visit and see what a relationship with Jesus is like? Do I belong in church because I'm following Jesus, or do I belong in church because it's easier for me to follow Jesus with other people? Perhaps it depends on how *belong* is defined.

In an effort to create some common ground, let's define the

term. The *Cambridge Dictionary* defines *belong* as "to be in the right place, or (of a person) to feel that you are in the right place."[1] The *Oxford Dictionary* defines *belonging* as "an affinity for a place or situation."[2]

Working from those definitions, I think we should be intentional about making room in church for anyone to attend and get involved so that it's easier for them to follow Jesus. As ethicist Stanley Hauerwas said, we should never offer belonging just because "it's a nice thing to do":

> Community for community's sake is not a good idea. Sartre is right: hell is other people! Community by itself cannot overwhelm the loneliness of our lives. I think we are a culture that produces extreme loneliness. Loneliness creates a hunger—and hunger is the right word, indicating as it does the physical character of the desire and need to touch another human being.[3]

The kind of belonging I'm putting forward not only counters loneliness but also connects people to God. Offering it doesn't require a shift in theology. I believe you shouldn't reconstruct orthodox doctrine to extend belonging to people, but you must do life *with them* and be *for them*.

THE CHURCH EXISTS FOR _____?

All this "belonging talk" might confuse you, get you excited about what's next, or lead you to think, *Foul! The church is for believers only!*

I'm sorry, but I'm going to make everyone mad with what I'm about to say: I don't believe the church ultimately exists specifically for believers or specifically for non-Christians. Let me explain. I'm fairly certain the Great Commission reminds Jesus followers to go and make disciples—aka, teach students and people (see Matthew 28:19–20). How does discipleship begin? By finding people who aren't following Jesus, investing in them, and then helping them grow so they can share him with others. Within that paradigm, the church makes disciples who invest in future disciples. In that sense, the church is not primarily for those who follow Jesus or those who do not.

So, who is the church for?

God.

The church is *for* God. It belongs entirely to him and exists to glorify him. Everything the church does should highlight God's fame and prestige. The church is comprised of Christians who should be equipping and encouraging one another to follow Jesus so they can help people find and follow Jesus *for God's glory.* Thus, the purpose of any church gathering is to glorify God.

Sadly, some struggle with the "help people find and follow Jesus" part. Many of us catch nasty spiritual viruses like "spiritual entitlement" or "legalism" or "holier than thou." Such viruses make us forget our past, our sin, and our potential to still commit terrible evils. Our false self-perceptions grow into toxic comparison as we measure our shortcomings against the flaws of others (which makes it easier not to share the gospel with "those people"). If we don't share, we aren't giving God what he desires.

In Philippians 2:9–11, Paul told us that God gets the most glory when people far from him become followers of him:

God exalted him to the highest place
    and gave him the name that is above every name,
that at the name of Jesus every knee should bow,
    in heaven and on earth and under the earth,
and every tongue acknowledge that Jesus Christ is Lord,
    to the glory of God the Father.

Sounds like an amazing worship service! Similarly, Jesus also taught three times in Luke 15 that God throws heavenly parties for those who were lost but are now found:

There will be more rejoicing in heaven over one sinner who repents than over ninety-nine righteous persons who do not need to repent. . . . There is rejoicing in the presence of the angels of God over one sinner who repents. . . . We had to celebrate and be glad, because this brother of yours was dead and is alive again; he was lost and is found. (verses 7, 10, 32)

God is enthralled when someone made in his image and likeness quits drifting from him and starts running to him. The ninety-nine usually get jealous of the prodigal's party, but they *have* to get over it! There's a lot of work to do! I believe that when Christians make room for anyone in church, they're actually making it easier for that person to learn about Jesus and follow him, thereby glorifying God. Helping non-Christians to experience a sense of belonging in a local church is not the same as pronouncing salvation onto them. It's easier to follow Jesus in community than in loneliness. We need more churches where people can *belong so they can belong.*

Churches need to be places where anyone can belong so they

can encounter Jesus and eventually join our Father's family! The answer to my friend's question from earlier in the chapter ("Does belonging precede life change, or do we belong because our lives changed?") is yes! Ask yourself the two questions we discussed in the previous chapter: "Who created them? Who died for them?" Everybody has the same intrinsic value. Everyone is someone God created and Jesus died for. They should feel welcome enough to attend a service, small group, or gathering before they believe or even if they don't agree with the church's position.

> Refusing to offer belonging not only robs God of his due glory but also hurts more people than we realize.

Creating environments and fostering attitudes where belonging precedes belonging hardly implies backpedaling in theology. It requires firm biblical convictions and strong leadership. It's not simple. Jesus, however, never invited anyone to *easy;* he called his disciples to *difficult.* Get ready for difficult, because Jesus's mission is one of self-sacrifice, character, strategic thinking, patience, empathy, bold conviction, and relentless love. Fear should never hold you back from helping foster communities in which anyone can find Jesus. Refusing to offer belonging not only robs God of his due glory but also hurts more people than we realize. To love people not like us requires power from One not like us.

Humans are relational beings. God created us to have relationships and live in community. God said as much in Genesis 2:18: "It is not good for the man to be alone." In her discussion of intersexuality, Dr. Heather Looy wondered if God's intentional differentiation of human genders is "a way of structuring into creation a basic need for us to be in relationship, so that it is in community, not individually, that we most fully reflect God's image and are most fully equipped for the tasks to which we are called."[4] It's easy to see why she would postulate such an idea, as we were made for relationships, and relationships depend on belonging.

Feeling left out can trigger toxic emotions such as feeling rejection. Can you remember a time when you experienced rejection? I'm sure you can, because it seems easier to recall pain instead of joy. Rejection invites other emotions like loneliness, sadness, anger, and depression. People look for belonging wherever they can find it. You already know stories about people who found a circle of friends, joined a gang, or got involved in a relationship because the thought of rejection was too much to handle. Thankfully, belonging is connected to more than just personal relationships.

BELONGING AND REJECTION

The concepts of identity, belonging, community, and faith are inseparable. In some way, each person's primary identity is tied to their primary communities. Your family, close friends, and individuals you spend time with either validate or challenge your identity. Whether or not a community makes room for others depends on the group's level of friendliness and authenticity.

In fall 2016, my wife's dad had an aortic aneurysm and dissection. His aorta literally started to split apart. He was rushed to the emergency room and into surgery less than an hour later. The operation lasted for hours. Our family was told that only a small percentage of people who undergo this surgery survive the following twenty-four hours. Thankfully, he survived and is back to his normal routine of life!

If surgery is a precise event, imagine how long *spiritual* heart surgery takes. How long did it take you to come to grips with Jesus? If you follow him, he's still performing spiritual heart surgery on you.

When God reaches into our hearts, removes our idols, deals with our insecurities, and refines our faith, it not only lasts for a while—it hurts! In an effort to avoid pain, we're tempted to stabilize our insecurities with our toxic habits. Continually aligning ourselves and identifying with Jesus is anything but simple.

If you're not already a little flustered by some of my ideas, this next sentence might do it: Ambiguity isn't always bad. Uncertainty that arises from not knowing how to love God and people at the same time creates personal ministry opportunities (specifically, ministry to people who are far from God or feel that he doesn't love them).

Some individuals who relate or identify as LGBTQ view church as the last place they are likely to experience belonging. They've been hurt by Christians or bad church experiences, or they've seen Christians hurt friends. Consider Lucy's experience:

> Growing up in the church has played quite a big part in these insecurities. The ultimate lowlight was confiding in a pastor about my sexuality when I was 18. He politely informed me that my feelings were from the devil, and went on to share our conversation—which I had believed to be confidential—with the church the following Sunday as part of his sermon on "sexual immorality."[5]

I'm sure Lucy felt humiliated, betrayed, and rejected. Something similar may have happened to you or someone you care deeply about. When I try to place myself in the shoes of both parties involved, I struggle to decipher what good the pastor expected to come from his treatment of Lucy. When she became old enough to decide if she would attend church, I bet she chose not to. Whatever belonging she had felt up to that point was probably gone or severely damaged.

People like Lucy might view returning to church as returning to their abuser. Observing the situation from their vantage point, one could understand their hesitancy. In community, we experience pain, but within another community, we can encounter healing and growth. Past experiences with religious weirdos may have hurt people, but God can use you to give them new experiences that will help them heal and grow. If people feel uncomfortable with Jesus because of bad experiences with Christians, *imagine how God could use good experiences with Christians.* Imagine how God might use you! It can make more of a difference in their lives than we know.

> If people feel uncomfortable with Jesus because of bad experiences with Christians, imagine how God could use good experiences with Christians.

This reminds me of two friends my mom had when I was growing up: Sandra and Janet. They were a couple and often joined my mom and Vera at parties and events. Every now and then, they'd even join us for a Friday-night dinner.

One particular evening as we were driving to a restaurant to meet Sandra and Janet for dinner, Mom and Vera were repeatedly telling me not to ask them questions. Those who know me understand that I'm very extroverted and always have been. For me to be quiet isn't the easiest task in the world! Still, I received their message and promised to listen more than talk.

I immediately failed when I saw Sandra. She and Janet had arrived before us and waved us over to their table. When we got to the table, I noticed that Sandra had a black eye.

"What the—?"

My mother's hand quickly went over my mouth before I could loudly finish my sentence. Vera and Mom gave me the look—be quiet or else!—that only parents can give. Sandra chuckled a little, smiled at me, and told my mom that it was okay. We sat down, looked at the menu, and ordered before discussing the elephant in the room.

Sandra told us that it had been quite the week. "On Monday, Janet and I went to the Bible study at this church we've been attending," she explained.

My mom interrupted her story. "A Bible study? That's your first problem."

"Mary Lou, please! Now's not the time," Vera objected, wanting Sandra to continue.

After a quick but awkward silence, Sandra went on. "As I said, we had been attending for a little bit and I really liked it."

This time Janet interrupted. "Well, I never liked it," she said in a stern voice.

"That's you, and we're talking about me," Sandra responded tersely.

Another awkward silence ensued while I fought the urge to tell a joke.

"Monday night after the study, the pastor asked to speak with us in her office. She had 'the talk' with us."

Mom and Vera both just shook their heads and offered their apologies. They had been recipients of "the talk" before. Many of the people in my mom's community called it that because you were told what the Bible said about homosexuality, that you were going to hell, and that if you didn't immediately repent, you couldn't attend the church.

Janet said she liked the fact that a woman was the pastor, but she never liked her or the other church leaders. "My life feels better without them."

"Yeah?" Sandra asked in an irritated tone. "My life doesn't. I liked this one."

To add insult to injury, a couple of days later, on Wednesday, Sandra was mugged. She had stopped at a fast-food restaurant to grab dinner for her and Janet. Two guys with guns stopped her as she was walking back to her car from the restaurant. They punched her in the face, smacked her in the back of the head with one of the guns, took her purse and food, and drove off with her car.

"I wish this all hadn't happened the same week. I haven't felt this alone in a while," Sandra bemoaned.

"You have us," my mom said, taking Sandra's hand.

"And me!" Janet added.

"I'm only here on the weekends!" I finally commented, which got a laugh out of Sandra and Janet.

"Thank you all, but it feels different when you have people surrounding you who share your faith."

I'll never forget those words: *it feels different when you have people surrounding you who share your faith.*

Sandra died in her sleep a couple of years later. It was sudden and unexpected. To this day, I don't know if she had ever found a church that was willing to journey with her. I wonder what would've happened if her and Janet's conversation with the pastor had gone better. In a couple of chapters, we're going to discuss the importance of having friends who relate as LGBTQ, listening to their stories, and dropping assumptions. For now, let's take a gander at the early church, because it serves as an example of what a "belong so they can belong" attitude looks like.

BEGINNING TO INTENTIONALLY OFFER BELONGING

Acts 1:8 isn't just the outline of the book of Acts; it's Jesus's parting instructions to his disciples: "You will receive power when the Holy Spirit comes on you; and you will be my witnesses in Jerusalem, and in all Judea and Samaria, and to the ends of the earth." Ever since Jesus spoke those words, the gospel has been heading to the ends of the earth. Obviously, the gospel's expansion isn't limited to Acts but is reflected through the New Testament in writings, leaders, and local churches.

The Early Church Didn't Exclude

In Acts 2, the church began with Jewish people from surrounding areas who were visiting Jerusalem (see verses 2–12). People became interested in Jesus and even trusted him while the first Christians assembled in homes and temple courts and met the needs of those in the community (see verses 42–47). Specifically, verses 46–47 might imply that unbelievers regularly spent time with believers: "Every day they continued to meet together in the temple courts . . . enjoying the favor of all the people. And the Lord added to their number daily those who were being saved." The church leaders seemed to value everyone, even Grecian widows.

While pastoring the church in Ephesus, Paul asked Timothy to choose elders who had good reputations with people outside of the church (see 1 Timothy 3:7). In similar fashion, he instructed Titus that elders "must be hospitable, one who loves what is good, who is self-controlled, upright, holy and disciplined" (Titus 1:8).

In Acts 8, Peter and others gave Simon the Sorcerer a chance when they were probably suspicious of him (see verses 9–25). In verses 26–40, Philip baptized an Ethiopian official who was a eunuch (and was probably looked down on). Later, in Acts 10, God told Peter to baptize a Gentile named Cornelius who was a Roman centurion. Though Peter's racist perspective made him reluctant to do so, he eventually obeyed God. (Paul later rebuked Peter for his racist perspective in Galatians 2:11–21.)

Cornelius was the first Gentile convert, and his baptism constituted a huge turning point—Paul was sent to share the gospel with the Gentiles. Shortly after, during the Council of Jerusalem, James said, "It is my judgment, therefore, that we should not make it difficult for the Gentiles who are turning to God" (Acts 15:19). It's almost as if every pivotal moment in Acts included offering belonging to people.

Churches Were Intentional About Attendees in Church Gatherings

Paul posed a hypothetical situation to the Corinthian believers about a worship service. This conjectural setting is often missed in the wake of debate about speaking in tongues. If Paul broached such a scenario today, he'd probably get blasted on social media, become fodder for blogs, and be the subject of YouTube videos! What would cause such a reaction? He created a scenario that had unbelievers attending a worship service and called believers to be intentional about who was and was not attending. In 1 Corinthians 14, Paul said,

> When you are praising God in the Spirit, how can someone else, who is now put in the position of an inquirer, say "Amen" to your thanksgiving, since they do not know what you are saying? You are giving thanks well enough, but no one else is edified. . . . So if the whole church comes together and everyone speaks in tongues, and inquirers or unbelievers come in, will they not say that you are out of your mind? (verses 16–17, 23)

Without question, Paul's example included his expectation that churches should be hospitable toward and intentional about unbelievers during church gatherings. Two words are significant to 1 Corinthians 14:16–24. First, *inquirer* (verses 16, 23–24) is translated as "a person who is relatively unskilled or inexperienced in some activity or field of knowledge, *layperson, amateur* . . . one who is not knowledgeable about some particular group's experience, *one not in the know, outsider.*"[6]

Second, *unbeliever* (verses 22–24) refers to someone who lacks faith and doesn't believe.[7] Regardless of how scholars differ in their interpretation of these two words, Paul was still describing people who didn't follow Jesus. And though a first-century worship service looked different from worship services in the last two hundred years, there's proof that Paul could have been discussing worship service:

- The literary context of 1 Corinthians 14 illustrates what their worship services entailed back then.
- Paul's use of the word *amen* is worship-service-type language.[8]
- He said that it's not good for unbelievers to leave a worship service confused or with no encouragement (see verse 17).
- His description of the whole church gathering together (see verse 23) is similar to how he described another worship service in 11:20.
- He talked about preaching when he mentioned the word *prophesying* (see 14:24).
- He desired that unbelievers would honor God as a result of what they experienced (see verse 25).
- He went into more detail about worship in verses 26 and following.

In the first century, it was probably a regular occurrence for unbelievers to be in church gatherings. As Paul referred to in 1 Corinthians 7:10–16, some marriages had believing and unbelieving spouses. I imagine some of those couples attended church together and may have even hosted a gathering or service at their house.

The fact that Paul wrote so much to the Corinthians about unbelievers made it all the more probable that unbelievers were attending church gatherings. Paul encouraged Christians in Corinth on scenarios involving unbelieving and believing spouses, how to relate with unbelievers, and meeting non-Christians where they were, and also instructed them on eating with unbelievers (see 1 Corinthians 7:10–16; 9:19–23; 10:27–33).

I'm speculating to some degree, but I think it's a realistic theory of how unbelievers were connected to early churches.

PUSHBACK AND DISCIPLINE

Before we move on, let me make some clarifications. First, I haven't meant to imply that everyone who relates as LGBTQ is an unbeliever. I'm merely showing how the early church intentionally offered belonging to *everyone* and did so without compromising biblical beliefs and the need for salvation. True belonging cannot exist without the boundaries that grace and truth provide.

Second, I'm not suggesting that a person's theological view of sex should be seen as "agree to disagree." God's creation of the marriage covenant, the power of sex, and the development of false identities are too profound to ignore. While a person can find Scripture to support views for various theological discussions, it's difficult to find Scripture in the Bible that supports sex outside marriage. A person will be even more challenged to find New Testament support for sex outside marriage.

I do not believe the serious nature of sexual sin should ever be downplayed. Sin needs to be killed. While all sin is equal in how it separates us from God, sexual sin and its consequences are uniquely dangerous. Paul specifically wrote about the seriousness of sexual sin in 1 Corinthians 6:18–20. He said that sexual sin is different from other sins for two reasons: sexual sin is committed against your body (which is the Holy Spirit's temple), and Jesus already purchased our freedom.

Paul reminded his readers (including future readers) that they were bought with a price—namely, Jesus's blood. No Christian belongs to themselves. Paul's train of thought was echoing Jesus's words in John 8:32–36, "You will know the truth, and the truth will set you free. . . . Everyone who sins is a slave to sin. Now a slave has no permanent place in the family, but a son belongs to it forever. So if the Son sets you free, you will be free indeed."

My goal here is not to excuse sin of any kind, nor is it to dumb down the truth. As I wrote earlier, I'm obsessed with trying to help churches to become places where people can find and follow Jesus well.

Some might ask, "What about church discipline?" Yes, there are times when church discipline is appropriate. When is that time? I'm not sure, but I do believe church leaders shouldn't be as trigger-happy with church discipline as many have been. I also believe that before disciplining someone, leaders should consider the other sins that are allowed without discipline.

If needed, church discipline should be done in love and should lead people toward restoration (see Galatians 6:1), as opposed to the unbiblical and harsh treatment some churches impose. It's tough to talk about disciplining people who haven't yet aligned with a church. Tougher still is to even consider correcting people we barely know. Church discipline should be a last resort, and it bothers me how quickly it's brought up in discussions.

> God doesn't throw parties over the ninety-nine; he celebrates the value of the one!

For now, remember that God doesn't throw parties over the ninety-nine; he celebrates the value of the one!

Since the early church intentionally offered belonging, shouldn't we do the same? If the first Christians invited people in who didn't believe, shouldn't we? If the early Jesus followers walked alongside individuals struggling with sin (which is all of us), how much more should we?

PART 2

COMPASSION FOR ANYONE

ACKNOWLEDGING OTHER PEOPLE'S EXPERIENCE

I met Rachel a few years ago when I spoke at her church. When she heard that I was making the trek from California to Illinois, she asked her pastor if the three of us could sit down and discuss some of her questions. So here we were, at a local coffee shop. Rachel didn't say much. She sat across the table from me, staring into her latte. The white foam had made what looked to be a perfect heart shape. But she wasn't staring at the heart. She was looking beyond it, through her coffee mug and into her past.

"Did you lose something in there?" I joked.

"What?" she asked.

"Your drink," I clarified. "You were staring at it so intently that I thought you lost something in it."

"I was just thinking about where I've been over the past few years," she replied.

I listened as Rachel briefly shared her story. She was raised by good parents, had a brother, and grew up in the church. Rachel wrestled with her orientation for a year. In her words, she went through three phases during that year:

No, I can't be gay to *I might be gay* to *I'm definitely gay.*

Right before Rachel came out, she met her future wife. They were married two years later. The couple moved to Arkansas and then to New York where they eventually divorced as a result of irreconcilable differences.

Following the divorce, Rachel made her way back to Illinois, moved in with her parents, and started dating another woman. She began attending her parents' church again, despite knowing the church was not affirming of same-sex relationships. She didn't know how the staff would react to her, nor did she know what to expect from the new senior pastor. Even though Rachel knew the church leadership probably wouldn't ask her to leave, she nervously waited for the "other shoe to drop" in some way. But that shoe never dropped.

One day Rachel emailed the senior pastor with personal and significant questions like, "Is there a spot for me at the table? Can I belong to this church?"

She began meeting with the senior pastor to discuss her questions and start a dialogue. Much to her surprise, the pastor never pressured her to conform to his belief about sexuality. He was very empathetic and honest about the church's theological convictions about sexuality and marriage. Their conversations covered everything from Jesus to sexuality to the purpose of the church.

Two critical events took place during this season. First, she left the woman she had been dating. Second, her church embarked on a study of the creation story. The pastor was eager to dialogue with Rachel about her thoughts on Genesis 1–2, so she started a deep study of the two chapters. While studying, Rachel was struck by some powerful observations: *I don't identify with Eve, but I'm created like her. What does redemption look like for me?*

As she thought more about Jesus, she noticed that he looks like God's perfect design for everyone. It wasn't long before she felt a battle of identities raging within her. Rachel wanted Jesus to be her primary identity. However, she came to terms with the fact that Jesus took a back seat anytime she entered a relationship. Rachel felt as if she would view any romantic relationship as an idol. She started to believe that God created marriage as a covenant relationship between a man and woman. She and the pastor began to read my book *Messy Grace*.

I was so intrigued by her story that we talked longer than the appointment was supposed to last. Before we were about to leave, Rachel commented, "I feel my life is very ambiguous right now. I'm confused about what's next and even more confused about who I am, but I have faith in who God is."

"And you have a good church," I added.

"Yes, I sure do," Rachel said and smiled at her pastor.

Rachel reminded me that some people will never step into your life until you allow them to do so *as they are*. Even today, she still attends the same phenomenal church where people love her not because of who she was or will be but because she's *Rachel*. They let Rachel be Rachel. She didn't have to pretend to be someone else. Her story illustrates how loving people well can make all the difference in the world.

Treating people well begins by doing two things: getting to know them and walking alongside them (as we discussed in the previous chapter). But how can we begin to do this? How do we love people where they are if we disagree with their relationship decisions or views on life? The solution never includes arguing them into a viewpoint; rather, it starts with acknowledging whatever reality they are experiencing and processing.

WHAT "ACKNOWLEDGING
AND ACCEPTING" MEANS

There's a difference between *acceptance* and *agreement*. Jesus followers must love people no matter what (acceptance), but they don't have to agree with their choices, affirm their theology, or approve their convictions (agreement). My acceptance of a person is based on who created them and who died for them. And *everyone* is someone God created and Jesus died for. My beliefs should never cause me to question someone's value.

Nevertheless, as society is increasingly plagued by false dichotomies such as "us versus them," many don't recognize the difference between acceptance and agreement. False dichotomies force us into either-or scenarios and people are quickly labeled as *affirming* (agreeing with same-sex intimacy) or *nonaffirming* (not agreeing). Because of this false dichotomy and the way religious extremists have treated LGBTQ people, inaccurate narratives are fabricated such as, *LGBTQ people are loved by affirming individuals and despised by nonaffirming individuals.*

> My beliefs should never cause me to question someone's value.

Ironically, plenty of same-sex couples and affirming individuals have close friendships with individuals branded as nonaffirming. To the dismay of both progressive and fundamentalist extremists, there are many people who hold an affirming view who happily attend nonaffirming churches. Why? Perhaps it's because they *relate* to their sexuality instead of primarily *identifying* as their sexuality (or an aspect of it). Those who primarily identify as LGBTQ see it as their main identity. As a result, they might see anyone with differing views on sexuality as harmful, bigoted, or perhaps even an enemy. It's tough to dialogue with such individuals because most protect their identity. Jesus followers should make *him* their primary identity because an identity rooted in Jesus is safe and secure in him. You don't have to fight to protect it. When your identity rests in Jesus, you're free to be an ordinary person through whom God does extraordinary things!

If people relate in some way as LGBTQ, then usually they view their sexuality as one aspect of who they are. As such, they are able to love people they disagree with and can still have deep relationships with them. They understand the difference between acceptance and agreement. Maybe they understand that part of the key to our disagreements is *acknowledgment.*

Acknowledgment validates others' experiences and notices their pain. It's very similar to or synonymous with *empathy,* which is, as author and professor Brené Brown says, "connecting with the emotion that someone is experiencing, not the event or the circumstance."[1] Brown also described empathy as the ability to "allow people to have feelings without taking responsibility for those feelings."[2]

Empathy isn't walking a mile in someone's shoes but rather walking miles next to them. Acknowledging others' reality isn't rejecting them or agreeing with their decisions or beliefs. Acknowledgment allows you to step into their lives and love them in the present moment. Those who are affirming and nonaffirming, people in same-sex and opposite-sex marriages, single individuals, and everyone else need to get better at acknowledging one another. The concepts of acceptance and acknowledgment both find their main foundation in loving others.

As I mentioned earlier, Jesus said the two most important commandments are to love God with everything and love people (see Matthew 22:37–39). Jesus referred to a portion of Leviticus 19:34 as one of the two greatest commandments: "The foreigner residing among you must be treated as your native-born. Love them as yourself, for you were foreigners in Egypt. I am the LORD your God."

Jesus's correct interpretation contrasted with that of the Pharisees' misinterpretation and the racist social norms of the day. Jesus *acknowledged* people no matter who they were, even if they didn't believe in him. Jesus utilized the Leviticus verse to show that to love people was not dependent on ethnicity, nationality, social standing, likability, or relationship decisions. In other words, love has no barriers.

> Empathy isn't walking a mile in someone's shoes but rather walking miles next to them.

Following suit, in the midst of a brutal empire with a sadistic and psychotic emperor, Paul told Christians in the city of Colossae to be strategic in their interactions with unbelievers: "Be wise in the way you act toward outsiders; make the most of every opportunity. Let your conversation be always full of grace, seasoned with salt, so that you may know how to answer everyone" (Colossians 4:5–6).

You could say that Paul was obsessed with how the attitudes of Christians could influence unbelievers for better or worse. He saw each moment with a person as an opportunity to build influence and eventually point to Jesus. Anything less than accepting and acknowledging will compromise influence we could have for Jesus. However, easier said than done, right?

UNDERSTANDING DEFINITIONS, DIFFERENTIATIONS, AND PEOPLE

Beginning to earn influence involves learning about who people are. Gaining insight about others isn't merely relying on our opinions. Hearing their stories, discovering how they relate to life, listening to their hopes and fears, and more helps us discern their self-perception. Remaining ignorant as to how individuals perceive themselves ensures that we'll have limited influence with them. Simply put, we cannot acknowledge another person's view of reality if we're clueless about who they are and how they interpret reality.

We can treat people well even if we don't know them, but we can treat them extremely well the more we know them.

Regarding the definitions of the following terms, I am not saying that I agree with the wording or that each one is accurate. It could be that by the time you read this, terms, definitions, and words deemed appropriate and inappropriate by society will have changed. The following definitions are short and intended to give you a snapshot of terms used in society. I do not intend to offend anyone, so if I do, I sincerely apologize in advance. My goal is really to show how varied the experiences and identities are of those in the LGBTQ community.

- *homosexual*—sexually attracted to one's own biological sex (now more of an umbrella word)
- *gender neutrality*—not referring to people by male or female sex but with neutral language
- *sexual orientation*—how someone is attracted and to whom

- *mixed-orientation marriage*—a marriage consisting of two people with differing sexual orientations
- *gender*—a synonym with biological sex, and there are times when the word *gender* is used to refer to social roles and constructs
- *gender identity*—the way an individual views and/or senses their personal gender
- *gender expression*—how a person's traits, outward image, and actions are associated with gender in a cultural context and regarding gender roles
- *gay*—usually refers to men who are attracted to men, but can be an umbrella word
- *lesbian*—a woman who is attracted to women
- *bisexual*—attracted to people regardless of their gender (or how they see their gender)
- *gender dysphoria*—emotional stress experienced from perceived misalignment between a person's gender identity and biological sex
- *transgender*—someone who perceives misalignment between their gender identity and biological sex
- *trans woman (transgender woman)*—a woman biologically born as male, who might experience gender dysphoria and/or decide to transition (hormone therapy and sex-reassignment surgery)
- *trans man (transgender man)*—a man biologically born as female, who might experience gender dysphoria and/or decide to transition (hormone therapy and sex-reassignment surgery)
- *ally/friends and family*—a straight person who supports the LGBTQ community

- *asexual*—experiences little or no sexual attraction to people
- *questioning*—people who are unsure of their orientation and/or gender and may or may not be exploring
- *queer*—can refer to people who are not heterosexual or cisgender and can also be used as a synonym for *questioning*
- *intersex*—born with both male and female biological and physical characteristics
- *pansexual/gender blind*—attracted to people despite their sex or gender
- *demisexual*—experiences attraction when a significant emotional bond emerges
- *two spirit*—used by Native Americans to describe people who have both male and female spirits (sometimes the words *soul* and *spirit* are used)
- *kink*—enjoying sexual expression outside what is considered the traditional expression of sexuality
- *sex-reassignment surgery*—an operation, usually combined with hormones, that a person undergoes to switch sexes
- *cisgender*—people who believe their gender aligns with their biological sex
- *nonbinary/genderqueer/pangender*—those who believe their gender is neither male nor female
- *gender fluid*—shifts between masculine and feminine
- *gender nonconforming*—sees gender identity as outside traditional masculinity and femininity
- *transvestite*—someone who likes to wear opposite-sex clothing (can be synonymous with cross-dressing but not synonymous with transgender)

- *affirming*—theological agreement with both same-sex and opposite-sex marriages
- *nonaffirming*—theological agreement with only opposite-sex marriage and sees sex outside of opposite-sex marriage as sin
- *Side A*—a same-sex-attracted person who believes God blesses both same-sex and opposite-sex marriages (some believe the Bible's words on sex and sexuality are not binding for today)
- *Side B*—a same-sex-attracted person who believes God blesses only opposite-sex marriage and that Christians relating as LGBTQ should remain celibate (some use the title *gay Christian* to relate with those who have similar life experiences)
- *Side X*—a same-sex-attracted person who believes Christians must fight to change their attraction to the same sex and thinks experiencing same-sex attraction is sinful or lightweight obedience

Again, some terms and definitions may not be worded as some people would prefer. They may not be as up to date as other lists, but you get an idea of the LGBTQ reality. Understanding where people are, who they are, and even the distinction of how people experience, think about, relate to, or identify with sexuality helps us acknowledge their reality and love them where they are.

No two people have the exact same thoughts, have made precisely the same decisions, or share identical experiences in any community. Likewise, not everyone relates as LGBTQ in the same way. For example:

- Some people are in same-sex relationships or marriages.
- Individuals may be sexually intimate in their marriage or they may not be.
- Sometimes a transgender man and transgender woman get married.
- Others are dating people of the same biological sex.
- Some individuals have dated people of the same biological sex but are in between relationships or may be unsure how to move forward.
- There are some individuals who are intersex.
- The suicide and attempted suicide rate for LGBTQ teens is staggering. The suicide and attempted-suicide rate for trans people is also staggering.[3]
- Some people have gender dysphoria but will never take hormones or undergo the sex-reassignment surgery, and others will and have.
- Over the years, more individuals who have had the sex-reassignment surgery have come forward to express their regret. Some wish to transition back, and some will, while others will not.[4]
- Some studies have shown an increase in attempted suicides of those who have undergone the sex-reassignment surgery, while other studies have not shown this.[5]
- Some people pursue relationships based on the gender to which they now relate.
- More married couples are open about discussing that either the husband or wife are same-sex attracted (commonly known as mixed-orientation marriages) but stay together because they love each other and want to honor the vows they made (and many are attracted to each other).

- Similarly, some people are bisexual and might be open to experiencing relationships with both sexes or choose relationships with the opposite or same sex.
- Some people may relate as asexual, which means they have little or no sexual desire.
- Many people are confused about their attraction or gender dysphoria and choose to keep it a secret out of fear of rejection or loneliness.

Some people might debate my premise that follows, but I'm going to state it anyway, based on real conversations I've had: some middle and high school students relate or identify as LGBTQ because they believe it to be trendy. Notice I said *some,* not all (this is not true of all students). I have had multiple teenagers come out to me as gay, bisexual, and so forth and then a couple of years later say they never really were. Nevertheless, there are teenagers who *are* same-sex attracted or experience gender dysphoria.

Acknowledging someone's experiences humanizes them.

That's a lot to think about, isn't it? Earning influence is difficult, which is why it's so easy to write people off. This is why acknowledging someone's experience is so important, especially as we get to know them. Acknowledging someone's experiences humanizes them. It helps us to accept people, love them well, and earn tremendous influence with them.

IT'S EASY TO BE JUDGMENTAL ABOUT OTHERS

One Sunday after I finished preaching, a woman and her teenage son approached me. "You should know that it's our last weekend at this church," she said with her arms crossed.

I was caught off guard, because just a couple of weeks earlier, this same woman sent me an email saying how much she appreciated the people in the church. I guess her opinion had changed.

She went on to tell me that she saw two men holding hands in the lobby and told a staff member but that individual chose to do nothing about it.

"Well, what are *you* going to do about it, Caleb?" she asked curtly.

"Nothing," I replied. She shook her head in disagreement.

Trying to reason with her, I asked, "What's the problem? You already know this church's theological conviction about marriage and relationships."

"My fourteen-year-old son doesn't need to see things like that. He's not used to it."

"Doesn't your son go to a Los Angeles public middle school?" I asked.

"Yes, but he doesn't see anything like that in his school! He would tell me if he did."

Immediately, I glanced at her son, who was looking at the floor to avoid making eye contact with anyone. Obviously, he had seen many "things like that" and was keeping what he saw at his public school a secret.

I theorized that her son probably saw more than what she knew and asked why she wouldn't want to take advantage of this opportunity to have a conversation with him about it. But, alas, she responded with more arguing, more finger pointing, and more promises of her departure from the church. Unfortunately, it was time to ask her a tough but loving question.

"Didn't you and your husband get an 'unbiblical divorce' not too long ago? Weren't you worried about being kicked out of the church? And didn't we promise to journey with you during this season of your life?"

Now she was silent.

"Might this be an opportunity to pay forward grace you've received?" I asked.

The good news is that she didn't leave the church. I knew this woman well enough to say what I did about the divorce, but her comments show the destructive power of assumptions. Making assumptions about people instead of getting to know them is a subtle and passive-aggressive way to reject them.

HOW TO BEGIN ACKNOWLEDGING SOMEONE'S EXPERIENCES

The majority of LGBTQ people I know are just like the majority of everyone else I know—they're afraid of rejection and loneliness. They long for intimacy that feeds their soul, yet in our society, sex is seen as the ultimate form of intimacy. And they attend churches that discuss marriage more than singleness (which describes the average church in North America). No one is set up to succeed in such a scenario. We need to acknowledge their reality and walk with them.

Get to Know People Who Relate or Identify Differently Than You

In Malcolm Gladwell's book *Outliers,* he asks, "Why is the fact that each of us comes from a culture with its own distinctive mix of strengths and weaknesses, tendencies and predispositions, so difficult to acknowledge?"[6] The less we know about people, the more indifferent we become. The more we know about people, the more we value them.

Former United States Supreme Court justice Lewis Powell once commented to a law clerk, "I don't believe I've ever met a homosexual."[7] Justice Powell was obviously not aware. One of his clerks was gay and actually told him, "Certainly you have, but you just don't know that they are."[8]

While I'm sure Justice Powell was a good guy, he could've done better. The more dialogue you have with people who relate or identify as LGBTQ, the better. The more conversations you have with same-sex couples, transgender teenagers, and those who are celibate because of theological convictions, the better. You'll empathize with them regardless of their perspective and even if you don't fully understand their reality.

People experience and process their sexuality in different ways. Author and speaker Rosaria Butterfield gives the following example: "One with SSA [same-sex attraction] may feel an oppressive, chronic loneliness, while the other may feel bitter envy about friends who have gone on to marry. It's vital when standing with a Christian in her

> The less we know about people, the more indifferent we become. The more we know about people, the more we value them.

grief—whether we feel that grief to be well earned or not—to try to see things from her point of view."[9]

As you get to know people, make relational investments in them. Meet with them, listen to them, serve them, pray for them, be more concerned about what they're enduring than what you're going through, and so on. Increased relational investments afford you more influence, and the more influence you have, the more your words carry weight. The more your words matter to the other person, the more you can inspire them to follow the source of their true primary identity: Jesus.

Dialogue About Differences

Let me say it again: this is a lot to take in. Really getting to know anyone is a complex process because everyone is different. Often our differences can tear us apart. Trying to immediately resolve ambiguity between you and others further divides us. On the other hand, the tension we feel between the divide can bring us together. Acknowledging our differences and seeking to understand them creates a bridge. If tension creates a bridge between two polar opposites, the bridge fosters more unity than division.

> When people lean in to understand those who have contrasting views, they move toward each other.

Tension not only creates a bridge between one side and the other but also grants an opportunity for dialogue. When people lean in to understand those who have contrasting views, they move toward each other. They begin listening, having discussions, and developing their empathy threshold. The bridge that tension builds will destroy false dichotomies that currently divide us. If you try to resolve ambiguity's tension, you lose the bridge! Tension is uncomfortable, but at least it brings us together. We can do life with one another in the uncomfortable middle.

Acknowledge the Bad Experiences

Everyone brings previous experiences into current relationships. Some of those experiences are filled with hurt, shame, guilt, wounds, and rejection. The negative issues in the past can dictate how a person interacts with and interprets others. This is why acknowledging a person's emotions, experiences, and thoughts is key. We should be asking ourselves questions like:

- How does _____ experience rejection as a result of their bad experiences?
- How does _____ experience love as a result of their good experiences?
- How does _____ relate to others because of their experiences?

Lesbians such as my mother and her partner have been mocked and cast aside because of their relationships. Gay men such as my friend Neil have been physically beaten just because they came out as homosexual. I'm sure I could tell more stories, but you have the gist of what I'd share. You've already witnessed a loved one's pain, heard the stories, read the articles, watched the reports, or seen the headlines. Some people bear the ugly burden of bitterness because someone they love was hurt. Shamefully, some of those who hate LGBTQ people have the audacity to refer to themselves as Christian.

While opinions of Jesus and Christianity have been damaged, followers of Jesus like you can show his love by acknowledging the reality and fostering authentic relationships with people. Each person's warmest memories and deepest pains have been forged in the context of their relationships. If bad experiences with Christians turned people away from Jesus, imagine how good experiences with Christians could help them walk toward him! Just picture how a person with bad religious experiences could be radically transformed by the power of a loving and redemptive community—*that's what happened to me!* You can be that Christian who loves them well, but it all depends on whether you're willing to be with people or not.

DISTINGUISHING PEOPLE FROM IDEAS

W hat should've happened?" That's the question Harry asked me, and I wasn't sure how to respond at the time. Five minutes earlier, I'd finished preaching the last service of the day at the church where Harry served as a backstage-tech volunteer. He had been at my side all weekend, so we got to know each other. I thought he was engaging and enjoyable, but there seemed to be an unspoken burden that he was carrying. I hadn't asked him about it, but when he approached me, he was upset. He told me that this was his last Sunday with the church and then told me why.

In Harry's mind, he had been living the American dream. He had a beautiful wife, two daughters, a good house with a reasonable mortgage, a top-tier management position at his company with future promotions awaiting him, and a church that his family loved deeply.

A few weeks earlier, Harry and Jan's oldest daughter (who was twenty at the time) came out to them. She told them three things: she had been attracted to women for as long as she could remember, she hadn't decided if she would pursue a relationship with a woman, and she loved Jesus very much. Harry and Jan were surprised and unsure of how to process this revelation but were committed to being fully present in their daughter's life no matter what. However, they were nervous about how their church leaders would handle the news.

Every now and then, Harry heard a harsh statement or two about those who made relationship choices that were contrary to historic Christian interpretations. When he heard such statements in the past, he would say an "amen" in his head, as no one close to him had ever identified as LGBTQ. But since his daughter had come out, everything was personal, and the "amen" in his head was fading away.

As best they could, Harry and Jan tried to reassure each other that although the leaders of their church were bold, they were also compassionate. It turned out that the couple had valid reasons to be nervous.

A few days before I had been scheduled to preach at this church, Harry's daughter came home in tears. Harry's heart sank because he was almost certain he knew why. Their daughter was a middle school small-group leader at their church. After the student-ministry groups had ended that evening, she decided to come out to the student pastor. After she told him the same three things she'd told her parents, he said that while their student-ministry group cared about her, she could no longer serve as a small-group leader for them. She was crushed. Apparently, it hadn't dawned on the student-ministry pastor to find out more about her story. She saw his dismissal of her with a smile as adding insult to injury.

The following morning, Harry headed to the church to have a chat with the student-ministry pastor. In the past, he had tried his best to let his daughter address her own situations, but this was different because it involved their family's church.

Harry arrived promptly at nine in the morning and stood outside the student-ministry building. The doors were locked, and as he peered into the window, there didn't appear to be signs of life.

"Figures," Harry grunted as he walked over to the church's main office. He opened the door and walked right past the receptionist. The church staff had become accustomed to Harry over the years. He was helpful and kind, and many correctly suspected that he was one of the more generous donors in the church. The receptionist welcomed him and thought it odd that Harry didn't return the greeting.

After walking through the office, Harry approached the door of his close friend on staff: the executive pastor. The two of them loved talking finances, operations, data analysis, all things Apple, and golf. Today, however, none of that mattered.

The pastor was surprised, almost annoyed, when he saw a figure just barge into his office. His attitude changed when he saw it was Harry. With a smile, he got up from his desk to greet his friend, but his smile quickly faded when Harry began to tell him of the previous evening's events with his daughter. Harry was shocked when the pastor said he heard what happened and fully supported the student pastor.

"She just recently told us," Harry pointed out, "but we listened. Why didn't your youth guy ask about her story last night?"

The pastor was unmoved and toed the party line in support of his employee. "Perhaps you should reevaluate your priorities and which voices you listen to on this matter. Scripture matters, Harry."

Without missing a beat, Harry replied, "Thank you. I'll do

just that. Consider this my last weekend serving on the tech team."

"Harry," the pastor said as Harry walked toward the office door, "you don't have to do this. We've known each other for years."

Quickly turning around, Harry retorted, "And I've known my daughter longer! Her whole life!"

"Harry—" the pastor began, but Harry was already walking out of the church office. To my knowledge, Harry and his family haven't been to a church since. My heart was grieved because everyone lost something in this circumstance and it didn't have to be that way.

> Christians need to move ahead of society by distinguishing people from ideas.

You could be thinking that story is too over the top to be true! I promise you, it is a true story. I wish I could tell you that I made this story up or exaggerated the details, but I would be lying (although, as you may have guessed, I did change people's names to protect their identities). However, I'll begin by acknowledging some things about the story.

There wasn't a ton of messy truth in this story. Harry, the student pastor, and the executive pastor all had biblical convictions about sex. However, the executive and student pastors both lacked compassion with Harry and his daughter. Whereas Harry and Jan took time to listen to their daughter's story, the executive and student pastors did not, therefore losing an opportunity to be compassionate. Neither pastor handled their conversations well. On the other hand, Harry didn't deal with the situation all that great either. He went to the church when he was still too emotional, walked right into the executive pastor's office, and immediately confronted him on the issue.

While Harry's side of the story is skewed toward his emotional attachment to his daughter, he was absolutely correct with how he defended his daughter. Also, I don't believe that the executive and student pastors should be stereotyped as villains. They lead a church with a large attendance, so each day is filled with people problems. (People make up the church, and people have problems. The more people, usually the more problems.)

Churches such as Harry's can do better. Actually, I need to rephrase that last sentence: *Christians can do better.* What do Christians who do better have in common? Perhaps the solution is found by reexamining Harry's situation and asking, *What should've happened?*

No one will join or regularly participate in a community until they feel a sense of belonging there. Yet, as we've touched on here and there, loneliness is painful. It drives us to find a community that will accept us. In order to help, Christians need to move ahead of society by distinguishing people from ideas.

THE POWER AND BATTLE OF IDEAS

In 1912, during a message he delivered for the opening of the 101st session of Princeton Seminary, a professor named John Gresham Machen said,

> False ideas are the greatest obstacles to the reception of the
> gospel. We may preach with all the fervor of a reformer and

yet succeed only in winning a straggler here and there, if we permit the whole collective thought of the nation or of the world to be controlled by ideas which, by the resistless force of logic, prevent Christianity from being regarded as anything more than a harmless delusion.[1]

A battle of ideas has ensued ever since humanity was separated from God. Unfortunately, in the recent history of the 1800s and beyond, many Western Christian leaders stopped publicly engaging in discussion over ideas on ethics, philosophy, life, and family. Why did they stop? It might be a result of ignorance, fear, arrogance, or guilt over sins like the slave trade or racism. One of the sad results of stopping was that many Christians began to mistakenly assume their worldview to have home-field advantage. Many public discussions about faith and culture didn't include the everyday person's needs or struggles. In one conversation, some Christians claimed to love God, while in another conversation they spewed racism, pro-slavery propaganda, the devaluing of women, and the destruction of native peoples. Ideas and opinions became more important than people. Regrettably, not much has changed today.

People or Worldviews?

Worldviews that prioritize ideas over people have always been easier to promote. An example of this is scientism, in which something is thought to be true and real only if it can be seen, touched, observed, and tested. Faith, unconditional love, miracles, the spiritual realm, and anything else that cannot be seen, touched, observed, or tested is seen as ridiculous. Scientism is a foundational worldview for society and the basis for many ethical and political views today. As Christian philosopher J. P. Moreland warns, Western society "has turned increasingly secular and the power centers of culture (the universities; the media and entertainment industry; the Supreme Court) have come increasingly to regard religion as a private superstition."[2] While God's values always run countercultural to the world, certain ideas make God's values appear foolish, controlling, and bigoted.

As Christians are experiencing today, *influence lost is influence hard to regain,* especially when our society is continually driving people to an elaborated view of self. Repeatedly, ideas such as the freedom to do whatever you want (as long as it doesn't hurt anyone) and viewing yourself and others however you want are prevailing.

Our sinful insecurities long to latch on to the next best idea or worldview that grants us what we desire most: ourselves as the pinnacle of our lives. Since every human has equal intrinsic value, everyone should be allowed the freedom to have personal opinions and make their own decisions. However, when someone follows Jesus, every decision in their life either belongs to Jesus or is heavily influenced by him. As we've learned, because we're made in God's image and Jesus died for us, we have purpose, identity, and value.

> Our sinful insecurities long to latch on to the next best idea or worldview that grants us what we desire most: ourselves as the pinnacle of our lives.

The late atheist and author Christopher Hitchens disagreed: "God did not create man in his own image. Evidently, it was quite the other way about, which is the painless explanation for the profusion of gods and religions, and the fratricide both between and among faiths, that we see all about us and that has so retarded the development of civilization."[3]

Ironically, while Hitchens's comments are directed at proving the ridiculousness of religion (made by humans), they actually reveal the ridiculousness of humanity when not in relationship with God. His comments also underestimate the power of community being united under the power of a loving God.

My friend Pastor Jason Caine and I often talk about the intersection of society and faith. More than once in our conversations, he has said something along the lines of, "People try to make an inclusive God exclusive to their own group. We idolize our group and demonize other groups."[4] We see this all too often in the faith community and in society as a whole. Sociologists call this idea *intergroup sensitivity effect*. The idea centers around how people feel personally offended when someone offends a community or group to which they belong. They take on insults and criticisms of their group as if they were being insulted themselves, especially if the critic is from outside the group.

It can be difficult to differentiate ourselves from a community we've identified with. You've felt this before, right? It's easy to be offended when someone insults our church, alma mater, family, sports team, company, nation, and so on. (By the way, I'm not insinuating that it's always wrong to feel offended when someone unfairly criticizes those you value, but it's troublesome to *always* be offended at such criticism.) People won't listen to a critique about their group unless they believe you have the group's best interests in mind.

Don't Reduce People Down to Your Opinion of Them

Ever heard someone say things like the following?

- "Guns kill people!"
- "The internet is bad."
- "Money is the root of all evil."

Technically, those sayings aren't true. I'm not making a political statement; rather, I'm pointing out that a gun is an inanimate object with no mind or will of its own; that is, it's not living. Likewise, the internet isn't bad, but what people might do with it can be horrible. Also, the apostle Paul never said that money is the root of all evil. He actually wrote, "*The love of* money is a root of all kinds of evil" (1 Timothy 6:10). That places the blame of evil on people, not a lifeless coin or paper. He finished the verse by emphasizing individual blame for evil and describes how that evil erupts in life: "Some people, eager for money, have wandered from the faith and pierced themselves with many griefs."

In the same way, influence in and of itself is not good or evil. Influence can help or hurt people. It depends on who holds the influence. Regardless of who they harm or misrepresent, toxic extremists use influence to achieve the purposes that they believe to be correct. Those who are truly committed to a loving devotion should make the most of influence to bring people closer to Jesus. But how can you tell one type of person from the other?

Loving devotion maintains an overabundance of love with boldness and kindness. It's never without grace and is certainly not devoid of truth. Loving devotion gives people the benefit of the doubt, promotes dialogue, sees the equal value of others, and stands up to injustice.

However, when influence is wielded as a weapon against assumed enemies rather than as a catalyst to help others, society will be damaged and stunted instead of healing and moving forward. This is the result of influence in the hands of toxic extremists. Those who give in to toxic extremism take sides between grace and truth. Such individuals might never mention sin when it comes to issues they are passionate about. However, they may insinuate that people who don't completely agree with their view are unloving or evil.

> Loving devotion maintains an overabundance of love with boldness and kindness. It's never without grace and is certainly not devoid of truth.

Toxic extremism stifles critical thinking, dialogue, and relationships. It promotes narrow-mindedness, creates false dichotomies, and needlessly demonizes anyone with opposing views. But I believe people are growing tired of extremism in any form. Just as individuals are weary of religious extremism, studies are showing that young Americans are becoming uncomfortable with overly progressive ideas about sexuality.[5] For instance, a study that was published a couple of years ago showed the percentage of eighteen- to thirty-four-year-old non-LGBTQ who are allies has dropped significantly (from 63 percent in 2016 to 45 percent in 2018). For that same age group, the study showed a 13 percent decrease of female allies and a 27 percent decrease of male allies.[6]

Now, I don't for one second believe that people are less affirming of gay men, lesbians, and so on. As a high school small-group leader, a parent of public-school kids, and someone who speaks at student events and conferences, I have observed that some students are growing tired of society's extreme focus on sex and sexuality. Mind you, I'm not a religious-extremist cultural fundamentalist. In addition to reading data from studies, I've arrived at this conclusion after numerous conversations with Christian students who consider themselves allies and affirming of gay marriage.

The likelihood for suicide of LGBTQ youth is a horror we need to pray about and get involved with. Too many Christians are unaware of—or worse yet, indifferent to—this tragedy. Regardless of their beliefs or sexuality, people need to know *and feel* that they're loved, they matter, and they have God-given intrinsic value. Biblical beliefs should never sideline anyone.

Although probably unintentionally, some toxic extremists have used the hurt of LGBTQ individuals as permission to label anyone with differing opinions as "dangerous" or as empowering LGBTQ self-harm. Yes, some nonaffirming individuals hurt LGBTQ people with their actions, words, and attitudes. Notice that I wrote *some* instead of *all*. Both affirming and nonaffirming toxic extremists use influence to achieve their purposes no matter who gets hurt. So what if many nonaffirming people don't cause LGBTQ individuals to commit suicide? So what if nonaffirming people have loving and positive relationships with people in same-sex relationships? Some nonaffirming people may share their view in a way that hurts LGBTQ people. Therefore, the broad-sweeping generalization that the "nonaffirming position harms LGBTQ people" must be made so we can protect everyone. The rationale is a willingness to lie and misrepresent anyone in order to save everyone.

But the broad-sweeping generalization will never solve anything, because it isn't true. Lies always compromise the power and outcome of any argument. The broad-sweeping generalization is not only dishonest but also wicked and selfish. Positioning oneself as a social-justice hero by exploiting others' pain and demonizing individuals who believe differently than us only makes society worse. People who use such tactics actually divide society even more. Healthy and helpful platforms of influence are never forged through divisive tactics.

Amid the Democratic presidential debates and social-media attacks in 2019, President Obama wisely encouraged people: "This idea of purity, and you're never compromised, and you're always politically woke and all that stuff. You should get over that quickly. . . . The world is messy. There are ambiguities. People who do really good stuff have flaws."[7]

He went on to say, "There is this sense sometimes of 'the way of me making change is to be as judgmental as possible about other people, and that's enough.'"[8]

How we respond to each other has to change.

"THEY" *ARE* OUT TO GET ME!

Not too long ago, I read a social-media thread in which a person warned other readers, "Don't be mistaken: the LGBTQ community is out to get you!" That's a completely ridiculous statement. Are there LGBTQ extremists unwilling to accept anything less than agreement with their self-perceptions, decisions, and opinions? *Absolutely!* Are there examples of efforts to attack people of differing beliefs? *Yes.* But let's talk about *you.* I seriously doubt an organized effort to "get you"—whether you are affirming, nonaffirming, or still figuring it out—actually exists.

Assuming that "they" are out to "get you" might cause you to treat everyone who disagrees with you about sexuality as "they." Not only is this assumption illogical and untrue, but it transforms you into a toxic extremist.

As discussed in a previous chapter, people experience, relate to, identify with, and view their sexuality in different ways, so please don't throw everyone in the same category. Believing that a whole community is "out to get you" will make you mistreat people in that particular community. You'll also mistreat anyone that reminds you of someone in that community. Assumptions make *you* the villain. People have more depth than our opinions of them.

> Assumptions make *you* the villain.

Harvard professor Arthur Brooks recognized that people are deeper than our assumptions: "Our public discourse is shockingly hyperbolic in ascribing historically murderous ideologies to the tens of millions of ordinary Americans with whom we strongly disagree. Just because you disagree with something doesn't mean such disagreement equates to hate speech or the person saying it is a deviant."[9] When you can't tell the difference between a person and their view, you automatically equate them as less than human. If a person is merely an idea instead of a person, you don't feel the need to be kind. Few people, if any, are gracious to an idea. Why would they be? An idea is a concept without physical form. I believe this is why many people in society are quick to compare their detractors to the worst proponents of the differing view. Even more horrible, it becomes easier to liken dissenters with Adolf Hitler, Joseph Stalin, Ted Bundy, Lord Voldemort, and so on. Viewing people as less than human makes it easier to strike at them. And as fallen humans, we need little prompting to exert our self-perceived authority or to exact revenge.

Dr. Martin Luther King Jr.'s words about his enemies have really challenged my thinking and convicted my heart. More than once, when preaching about racist and prejudiced people, Dr. King implored his listeners to "not seek to defeat or humiliate the enemy but to win his friendship and understanding."[10] Mind you, I'm not referring to any LGBTQ individual, nonaffirming extremist, or affirming extremist as the enemy. But, as I've driven home, at times our pain, insecurity, misunderstanding, and yearning for justice can make us feel they are enemies, so Dr. King's plea certainly applies to our discussion. We must learn to love those with whom we fervently disagree.

Less than a week before his assassination, Dr. King said the following in a sermon: "There comes a time when one must take the position that is neither safe nor politic nor popular, but he must do it because conscience tells him it is right."[11] I had been working remotely with a ministry organization in a well-known city for a few weeks when a hate group (who claimed to be Christian) protested in that particular city against LGBTQ individuals. I contacted some pastor friends there and asked them what they were going to do. My suggestion was to stand across or down the street from the hate group while peacefully holding up signs that read, "God loves you."

Much to my dismay, every single one of my pastor friends said they were advised against doing so. They opted to meet in a nearby church and pray. I asked them to reconsider, pointing out that even just one of them holding up a sign would communicate a strong message. I'm sure it would have meant something to LGBTQ individuals who were there in response to the hate group. After all, our societal system expects Christian leaders *not* to do this, so a loving counterdemonstration would have been noticed.

I'm pro-prayer, but I can physically stand next to someone and pray at the same time. In this situation, I believe some pastors with good character made assumptions about the situation and missed an in-person opportunity to acknowledge the reality of hurting people.

I contacted my friend Cindy, who is in a relationship with another woman and lives in the city where the protests were taking place. She had been standing on the other side of the street from the hate group.

"What would it have meant to you if nonaffirming Christians stood next to you or even down the street holding up signs about God's love?" I asked.

"Seriously?" she responded. "It would've meant a lot. But come on, Caleb. People who can't bear the thought of my marriage wouldn't be caught dead standing next to me."

In her mind, the lack of Christians on that day proved her assumptions to be correct. I began thinking about what might have happened if even one pastor or Christian could've shown up that day—just one! The words of my favorite poet, Maya Angelou, echoed in my mind: "One person, with good purpose, can constitute the majority."[12] Usually, there are few times in life when you get the chance to be that "one person" to help someone else.

It's no secret that of the most hurtful things Dr. King endured was the apathy of his white Christian brothers and sisters who were silent. In private conversations, they fully supported the equality of races, but they were nowhere to be seen in the public spotlight. More than once, Dr. King lamented the indifference:

"It may well be that we will have to repent in this generation. Not merely for the vitriolic words and the violent actions of the bad people, but for the appalling silence and indifference of the good people who sit around and say, 'Wait on time.'"[13]

When Christians remain silent out of fear of what others will think, they compromise pivotal moments in which they could have made a difference in the lives of others. People are not ideas to hate. No matter who is being hated, believers must consistently acknowledge that hate is evil and stand against it. Doing so doesn't require you to change your beliefs about sexuality and relationships. So, if you have a chance to visibly stand against hate, take that stand. Cry with a family in their living room, listen to a person's story in the coffeehouse, stay on those long phone calls, go with someone to church, and pray for those in need.

Stand up to hate.

Love, pray for, and walk alongside the hated.

Love and pray for the haters.

HELPING OTHERS THINK EMPATHETICALLY

I had just finished preaching the second service at the church Dorothy and Janice had been attending for a few weeks when they walked up and introduced themselves to me in between services.

"Fine sermon," Dorothy complimented.

I thanked them and went on to ask their names, where they were from, and how long they had been attending the church. During our initial small talk, I also discovered they were Kansas City Chiefs fans, so obviously they were good people.

"What denomination is this church?" Janice asked as she looked at some brochures from the information table.

I answered their question and told them some of the good things I had experienced at the church.

"So, let's get down to brass tacks," Janice suggested. "We're in a relationship. Are we wanted here?"

"Of course you are!" I reassured them.

Janice clarified her question: "Well, more specifically, how would people feel about lesbians like us attending this church?"

"As far as I know, there are lesbians who attend here. There are also straight people, gay men, a few Cowboys fans, and one or two Bon Jovi fans who attend the church."

"Good to know," Dorothy said and then chuckled.

"We're Christians," she continued, "and we want to find a place where the people will love us for who we are instead of rejecting us for the relationship we're in."

"I want to have this conversation with you," I answered. "But more than that, I want to hear your stories and find out about what God is doing in your life. Would you be willing to meet with me tomorrow or the next day?" I asked.

"Sounds good!" Dorothy replied.

The next day, I was sitting in a church office with both of them. In the time we spent together, I discovered they had lived together for more than twenty years, weren't married, resided in the same house, slept in separate bedrooms, and were no longer sexually intimate. So, were they sinning? If they weren't having sex, were they sinning? My biggest challenge to them was asking why they introduced themselves as lesbians before they ever shared that they were Christians.

Near the end of our conversation, I explained the church's belief about sex and marriage and gave examples of how church staff and attendees consistently valued people. I also promised that if they attended the church for a few weeks, they would discover two things: the attendees had varying beliefs on several issues, and this was a safe place where theological agreement wasn't a precursor for valuing people.

"A new six-week sermon series is beginning next weekend," I shared. "If you're able, try to make it a priority to attend one of the weekend services for the next six weeks. The more time you spend at a church, the more you'll learn about it."

They agreed. The last time I checked, they were still attending that church. I tried to show empathy to Dorothy and Janice. Empathy places everyone on the same level. A positive relationship with us is part of the empathy that we should show. Empathy within community fosters healthy spiritual experiences that God can leverage to heal pain, communicate value, and even change perspectives, especially when emotional pain is involved.

Ralph Waldo Emerson said it well: "Our faith comes in moments. . . . Yet there is a depth in those brief moments which constrains us to ascribe more reality to them than to all other experiences."[1] Though the combination of our relationships, faith, and experiences can feel messy, I believe they lead us to truth. As we continue on our journey of messy truth and learning how to foster a community where anyone can feel loved, I want to help you create moments and experiences in community that influence people for Jesus. Specifically, I hope you'll saturate your community with individuals who feel rejected or who dislike Christians because of disagreements about sexuality. I pray that with a messy-truth perspective and a loving community at your side, your example convinces people to believe God isn't against them and that church is a place for them.

> No one comprises the church on their own, no one spiritually matures on their own, and no one undertakes Jesus's mission on their own.

You can't do this on your own. No one comprises the church on their own, no one spiritually matures on their own, and no one undertakes Jesus's mission on their own. You need other Christians to come alongside you. But first you need to help other believers see the importance of acknowledgment, acceptance, and loving others—in other words, *empathy*. It's your job to inspire them to biblical empathy. After all, it's what Jesus did.

IT'S WHAT JESUS DID

No one has ever shown more empathy than Jesus. As a matter of fact, empathy is how Jesus began his time on earth. When teaching the church in Philippi about humility, Paul wrote the following words about Jesus:

> He made himself nothing
>> by taking the very nature of a servant,
>> being made in human likeness.
> And being found in appearance as a man,
>> he humbled himself
>> by becoming obedient to death—even death on a cross!
>> (Philippians 2:7–8)

Jesus had the full human experience: childhood, adulting, relationships, and just doing life with people. Actually, that's an understatement; he took people almost wherever he went and used community as a vehicle for teaching, calling, comforting, and serving. And Jesus taught his disciples to love anyone and everyone:

- When he called his disciples to follow him, I'm pretty sure they weren't Christians yet and they had multiple flaws.
- Jesus allowed Judas to follow him even though Jesus knew betrayal was to come.

- Jesus allowed Judas to join him at a table even when Satan went into Judas's heart.
- Jesus loved Judas—deeply. He loved him despite knowing what Judas would do and that he would never repent.
- Jesus was criticized for hanging out in the middle of Matthew's tax-collector-and-sinners party, where conversations were probably worse than ones in a crowded church parking lot on a Sunday morning.
- In Matthew 5:38–48, Jesus told his listeners not to be haters but to give away their clothes for the sake of peace, choose humility over revenge, love and pray for their enemies, and go the extra mile for the sake of a relationship with someone the social norms tell them to hate.
- He crossed social and racial barriers when he treated a Samaritan woman with dignity (and ensured that his students saw him talking to her).
- It didn't worry him if someone questioned the legitimacy of his character or calling when he allowed a woman to wash his feet with her tears.
- Even when the Old Testament law said to do otherwise, Jesus was willing to forgive a woman caught in adultery.
- Jesus ate with Zacchaeus, a lowly and despised tax collector.
- In the parable of the good Samaritan and the parable of the banquet, Jesus defined neighbor as *anyone*.
- Even though the Pharisees hated Jesus, he met with Nicodemus late at night, ate dinner at other Pharisees' houses, and refused to allow the Pharisees to stone the woman caught in adultery (see John 8:7–8) despite having every right to as the sinless Son of God.

It never fails to amaze me that Jesus not only said and did these things but also lived them out with impeccable grace and truth. Hebrews 2:17–18 describes how and why Jesus is empathetic even now:

> For this reason he had to be made like them, fully human in every way, in order that he might become a merciful and faithful high priest in service to God, and that he might make atonement for the sins of the people. Because he himself suffered when he was tempted, he is able to help those who are being tempted.

Such grace and truth provided humanity with loving boundaries.

VIEW GOD'S GUARDRAILS AS BEING FOR THE BETTERMENT OF HUMANITY

Author and atheist Sam Harris claimed that Christians "tend to view sexual conduct as morally problematic and attempt to regulate it, both to encourage fertility and to protect against sexual infidelity."[2] As much as I want to disagree with Harris, there are definitely Christians who serve as the poster children of what he inferred. In his book *Letter to a Christian Nation,* Harris chided conservative believers: "Efforts to constrain the sexual behavior of consenting adults—and even to discourage your own sons and daughters from having premarital sex—are almost never geared toward the relief of human suffering."[3]

Again, I agree with Harris. Rarely does the average Christian ever discuss how God's guardrails regarding sex make society better. Part of being empathetic with others about sex and sexuality isn't just being firmly grounded in God's truth; it's also believing that God's guardrails make life better . . . *because they do.*

Imagine for a moment that sex was never taken outside marriage. Personally, I think little, if any, sex trafficking would occur. The world would be a place where sex wasn't a bargaining chip or used for power over others. Affairs would be long gone. I doubt pornography would exist. There would be no STDs. Instead of "what not to do" or "anything goes," society's main discussions regarding sex could be focused on how it enriches relationships, provides security, and enhances communication.

I know the world I'm describing isn't real, but that doesn't mean the world couldn't be a little better if each of us, one by one, decided to trust that God's guardrails are for the best, even when we may not agree with them. Living within God's guardrails isn't easy but living outside them quickly causes fear and chaos. And the more fearful we are, the harsher we become.

REPLACE FEAR WITH NAMES

It's easy for toxic fear to control us. As a matter of fact, when we don't understand a group, person, or idea, it's natural to become scared. Toxic fear disfigures our view of people so much that we can begin to believe that others don't possess dignity, passion, or depth. But, as I've said before, shallow people don't exist! Everyone has a soul, a name, and a story. Each person has what they believe to be good reasons for the opinions they have, values they believe in, relationships they've been in, and decisions they've made. It's easy to be indifferent toward, ignore, attack, or feel threatened by people whom you know next to nothing about or have been hurt by. Sometimes it's as simple as tuning into our favorite news outlet or talk show to hear them blast the people we don't know. It's a quick and lazy fix to let the outrage culture determine our view of others. Again, Arthur Brooks explains our situation well: "We are in our current mess of tribalism and identity politics not because of de-platforming or social media siloing—those are symptoms of the real problem, which is our attitude of contempt toward others."[4]

> When you replace fear with names, your view begins to change.

As you get to know those who are different from you—whoever that might be—toxic fear begins to fade. When you replace fear with names, your view begins to change. You start to realize some differences and things you never knew. Those who were once distant from you start to appear human to you. You can learn things like these:

- Not every lesbian sees that as her primary identity, just as not every gay man views the world mainly through the lens of his sexuality.
- Many individuals who experience gender dysphoria will never take cross-sex hormones or undergo surgery.
- More often, people in same-sex relationships and marriages are attending churches that have differing views of marriage.
- There are people in same-sex relationships who still believe that marriage is between a man and woman.

- Not every person who is same-sex attracted supports same-sex marriage.
- There are lesbians, gay men, and asexual individuals who consider themselves conservative Republicans or Libertarians.
- Some gay men and lesbians are at odds with transgender individuals, and a few are even very vocal about it.[5]
- Many people in same-sex relationships have never been to a pride rally or parade. A majority are not self-anointed social-justice warriors and are as frustrated with politics and society as anyone else.
- Not every transgendered individual is easily triggered or wears their feelings on their sleeves.
- And we could keep going . . .

Assumptions become prominent when empathy is absent. You assume less when you care to understand more. You care about anyone you empathize with, and empathy begins to change your perspective. Before your very eyes, you'll start seeing "those people" transform into living, breathing human beings. They won't be masterminds scheming to take away your rights, or henchmen who joyfully lure your child into wickedness. No, now they'll have names like Brie, Luis, Sofia, and Terrell. They'll drive regular cars, make house payments, want to attend certain schools, have worries about the present, and foster hopes for the future. Each of them has a story, and each story is intertwined with the stories of others. In a way, showing empathy to those different from you also shows empathy to people they are connected with.

SAVE A SEAT AT THE TABLE FOR THOSE
DIFFERENT FROM YOU

Now, you probably already know this, but allow me to say it anyway. Here's a burdensome fact about being empathetic—it only increases the tension you feel between grace and truth, which is uncomfortable because tension is uncomfortable. For instance, I fully affirm the differentiations between males and females as presented in Scripture. I also want to be compassionate toward those who experience dissonance between their biological sex and gender. Though I've never experienced gender dysphoria, I know that I can walk next to people along life's course. My empathy for others doesn't come at the expense of Scripture, but with the support of Scripture.

So, as we seek to show empathy, how can we start getting to know people? What does it look like to graciously engage someone's experience in a conversation? How can we help our friends and families to be more empathetic? Well, good questions are the best starting point . . .

ASK GOOD QUESTIONS

The late Dallas Theological Seminary professor Howard Hendricks was a tour de force. He taught and even mentored many students who went on to become tremendous ministry leaders, including Tony Evans, Andy Stanley, Priscilla Shirer, David Jeremiah, Bruce Wilkinson, J. P. Moreland, and Chuck Swindoll. Dr. Hendricks is probably most well known for his dynamic teaching style and understanding of how to study the Bible. With his son William Hendricks, he outlined his whole Bible-study method in *Living by the Book*. I believe that, to date, it's one of the best books written on Bible-study methods. Read their book and you'll find the pages are filled with questions. Hendricks was actually very up-front with his fondness of questions and said in the beginning of the book, "If you want to understand a biblical text, you've got to bombard it with questions."[6]

Hendricks was spot-on, and I'd like to borrow his phrase and adjust it a bit for our purposes: if you want to understand someone, you've got to ask good questions.

I believe that *questions* form a cornerstone of empathy. It's difficult to be empathetic without good questions. You won't learn much about the other person. Without good questions, circumstances and people remain mysteries. Refusing to ask good questions not only produces wrong answers but also ensures bad perspectives. You'll start heading in the wrong direction, and each step will place you further away from a solution and distances you from people you care about.

Asking good questions helps you to

- process the problem or circumstance
- develop a well-rounded perspective
- see assumptions, motives, and reasoning
- determine the emotions that are in play (for example, fear, worry, and anger)
- provide intentional responses instead of impulsive reactions
- bring down someone's guard
- foster empathy

- move toward the goal
- show others that you care enough to ask

Now, before we go any further, I need to make a confession (lest you think I'm an expert in asking questions). For most of my life, I haven't even attempted to ask good questions. Thinking through and developing helpful questions hasn't been my forte. Actually, I'm the polar opposite. I'll charge the hill without much discussion—fire the gun now and check the aim after. Unfortunately, when I've charged the hill with few or no questions asked, I eventually fall down the hill before reaching the top!

I started studying how to ask good questions because I became afraid of not asking questions or asking the wrong ones. I'm still not the best question asker, but I am getting better at it. Most people don't have an innate ability to ask good questions; rather, it's an art you develop. Anyone can become a better question asker. It just takes time. You need to ask better questions to think more deeply about people. Here are five tips to get you started.

1. Listen to How Others Ask Questions

If you want to ask good questions, then listen to podcast interviews or watch talk shows (that aren't annoying). You'll get better when you surround yourself with good questioners. Podcasts I listen to that have insightful questions are *HBR IdeaCast, Parent Cue Live, The Carey Nieuwhof Leadership Podcast, The Productivity Show, The Table Podcast* (Dallas Theological Seminary), and *unSeminary*. Regularly listening to people who ask good questions gets you in the mindset of doing so yourself. Take notes on how they do it. Ask yourself:

- How do they begin their questions?
- What words do they use most often in their questions?
- What words don't they use?
- How do their questions align with their interviewee's comments?
- What do all their questions have in common?
- How are the questions helpful?
- How do the questions draw out helpful information from the interviewee?

2. Study the Person and the Circumstance

It might be that you want to ask someone a series of questions. My advice is to think about the individual and circumstance you are dealing with. Are you tackling a subject that is personal for them? Is the issue personal for you, and if so, do they know it? Why is it personal for you? What emotions surround the context of the circumstance you're studying? How does the other person normally respond to questions? Are you having the conversation in an environment that allows for concentration?

These are just a few examples of questions that can help engage a conversation. Asking questions can even help you develop better questions.

3. Be Intentional with Your Words

Closed-ended questions can be answered quickly and with *yes* or *no* answers. Open-ended questions push the person to pause, think, process, and engage with the individual or circumstance the question is concerning. Words like *might* open up possibilities. Using words like *why* in certain questions take us backward into the past and can be far too ambiguous. Our intentionality in choosing helpful words for questions moves the conversation forward so we can linger on it. Notice the difference between the following three questions:

- Why did you make the same mistake again?
- In the future, how might you avoid the same outcome?
- How might I help you avoid the same outcome next time?

The second and third questions aren't perfect, but at least they move toward a solution rather than merely focusing on the past. As you can see, words matter.

4. Practice in Order to Make Perfect

Prepare for the conversation by writing down your possible questions. Look at them, let them sit, and reword them. Say them out loud and notice how they sound. Ask someone else the questions and get their feedback. Have spare questions at the ready.

If you want to practice your question asking, read Miguel's words below and write down some questions you'd have for him:

I feel that if I wasn't gay I wouldn't be as sensitive to people—to the needs of people and to the hurt that people have. I feel that all of this is from my gay side. . . . I look at a tree blowing in the wind and see more than just that. I see the symmetry of the tree. I see the leaves as they shimmer. You know. And I think those are all part of my gay nature, a sensitive, more tuned-in side of me. . . . I accept being gay and I really value it—you know, as something very important to me. . . . But I just go through this dilemma of what is the purpose of my life as a gay person if I'm already condemned.[7]

Make sure your questions are not aimed at trying to change the person but rather at getting to know them or understanding the situation. Such questions convey value of and concern for the other person. Dr. Henry Cloud wrote that "people feel cared about, and trust is built, when they know that we have a genuine interest in knowing them, knowing about them, and having what we know matter."[8] Few things build influence like helpful questions that express love and concern.

5. Ask Yourself and Others Questions

Following are some questions for you as you grow in empathy and attempt to lead others to be more empathetic. Obviously, some of these questions are for you alone. Others are designed to be for the people you are helping think empathetically. There are also questions that might be helpful as you have discussions with LGBTQ people who believe differently than you on subjects like sex and marriage. These questions also might be useful for discussions in small groups, Bible studies, and staff-team meetings.

Questions for yourself:

- Who do you know that is same-sex attracted?
- How long have you known them?

- Where and how did they come out to you?
- What were your feelings after you found out?
- Did their coming out change how you viewed or felt about them? Why or why not?
- What is your relationship like with family members, friends, and coworkers who are gay or lesbian?
- How can you be more intentional about your relationships with them?
- What causes assumptions?
- In the past, what assumptions have you made about people and their sexuality?
- What assumptions could you be making right now?

Theological questions:

- Why do you believe or not believe that God designed sexual intimacy to be expressed in a marriage between one man and one woman?
- Why have you maintained or changed your beliefs about sexual intimacy and marriage?
- Specifically, what do Jesus and biblical authors like Paul, John, James, Peter, and Jude say about sex and relationships?
- What are some ways to trust what Jesus says when our feelings tell us not to?
- What does Jesus require of your sexuality?
- How might a transgender man or woman feel about Genesis 1:26–28?
- How might gay men or lesbians feel when they read passages like Genesis 2:24?

- How does your theology empower your love for others?
- How can you notice when your beliefs cause you to be less loving?
- How are your biblical beliefs affecting the way you love others?

Questions about your church or community:

- What is your church's official or unwritten belief on issues pertaining to sexual intimacy, sexuality, marriage, relationships, and gender?
- Why do people who are attracted to the same sex or who are in same-sex relationships attend your church? Why have some left?
- How do LGBTQ individuals who don't attend your church view your church?
- If your church is nonaffirming, why do LGBTQ individuals and people with affirming views attend?
- What is your church's reputation in the local community?
- How were individuals treated when they left your church?
- How have Christians in your church hurt (even unintentionally) people who relate as transgender, gay, and so on?
- Do any amends need to be made? If so, what?
- How do your church leaders support LGBTQ visitors and attendees who are single because of their theological convictions?
- How do your church leaders love those who have not chosen celibacy?

Family questions:

- If you're married, are you and your spouse in agreement on sex, sexuality, marriage, relationships, and gender? Why or why not?
- How can you make your spouse feel loved and special?
- Do your children trust Jesus and attend church? Why or why not? If your kids do not attend church, how can you help them attend or find a church that resonates with them?
- What conversations have you and your children had about sex, sexuality, marriage, relationships, and gender?
- How can you plan to have more conversations in these areas with your kids?
- What are your kids learning in school regarding sex? How are you dialoguing with them about what they're being told?
- Do your kids feel the freedom to ask you questions? If not, how can you create that freedom for them?
- Who do your kids hang out with? Do they have a boyfriend or girlfriend?
- How can you partner with your kids' small-group leaders (or Sunday school teachers) to help them follow Jesus well?
- What can your family do to spend more time together?

Questions aimed at getting to know someone:

- How is _____ feeling?
- How can you help _____?
- What can you do to make _____'s day brighter?

- What do you appreciate about _____?
- Where has _____ come from?
- What do you have in common with _____?
- How has _____ experienced rejection in regard to their sexuality or relationship decisions?

Questions to help with empathetic thinking:

- How do others feel when you're listening to them? Do they feel listened to?
- Instead of just establishing rules, how do God's guardrails help and protect us?
- What bias do you have against someone that's holding you back?
- What do people hide from you because they don't feel safe around you?
- Think back to a time when you felt rejected. What happened? How did it feel to be rejected?
- Now think back to a time when you felt like you belonged. What happened? How did it feel to belong?
- What can you do to help your community love others well?
- How does it feel for gay men, bisexual teenagers, or individuals questioning their own sexuality to attend your church or study?

More questions for personal reflection:

- How are you currently identifying with Jesus more than with anything else?

- What can you do today to deepen your relationship with Jesus?
- Does your character afford you the credibility to journey with someone?
- How are you inspiring others to live in the tension of grace and truth?
- Do you need to apologize to anyone because of how you treated them in the past? If so, what is your plan to make amends?
- Where do you need to personally grow so you can have better conversations about Jesus?
- How can you consistently make your family members feel loved?
- Are you being led more by what you know or how you feel?

Questions surrounding current events (noting that the word *this* describes the event you're discussing):

- What happened in this particular circumstance?
- What is society saying about this?
- What are your friends and family saying about this?
- If you were _____, how might you feel about this?
- How did some people handle this scenario well?
- How was this not managed well? How could this have been dealt with better?
- What can you do to focus more on Jesus than on society's trends?

Deeper questions:

- How is identity at the center of this whole conversation (as well as the root of society's issues)?
- Do you believe everyone is sexually broken? Why or why not?
- How should people respond to new beliefs in light of their current reality?
- How can you best value people over your perceptions?
- Are you more worried about clarity or love? Why?
- How do you respond if someone is offended that you disagree with them over their relationship choices?

The better questions we ask, the more we connect with people. The more we connect with people, the more they feel loved and cared for. The more they feel loved and cared for, the higher the trust they place in us. The higher the trust they place in us, the greater our influence with them. The greater our influence with them, the more opportunities we have to share Jesus.

PART 3

CONVERSATIONS WITH EVERYONE

DO YOU HAVE THE CREDIBILITY
TO WALK WITH OTHERS?

So far we've discussed convictions about God's words and compassion for anyone. When examining our conviction about God's words regarding sexuality, we've discussed the value that God has assigned to each person, the fact that God placed guardrails around sex because marriage belongs to him and he loves us, and that while the church is comprised of only believers, God doesn't want only believers to hear about Jesus. He's most glorified when those far from him decide to follow him.

Then, with the value of people, guardrails around sex, and opportunities to share Jesus in mind, we talked about compassion for anyone. Specifically, we discovered that acknowledging the experiences of others is a chance to walk alongside of them, failing to distinguish people from ideas results in treating some people as less than human, and helping those around us to become more empathetic is a strong testimony to Jesus.

Now, we turn our attention to what's probably the most difficult guidepost of messy truth—conversations with everyone. How do you have helpful and truthful conversations? What about when you have to lovingly confront someone or ask them some crucial but uncomfortable questions? Better yet, what can you do to prepare for discussions like these? Where should they take place? What should you say or not say? How should you phrase tough truths you want to share? What does it look like to keep another person's perspective in mind?

We're going to dive into these questions and more, but first the launch pad for our conversations—character and integrity.

DISNEYLAND WITH BRIAN

If our family is not at home, chances are we're having fun at Disneyland or Disney California Adventure. We are regulars on Main Street, in Star Wars: Galaxy's Edge, and on rides like Soarin' Around the World. One day when we were waiting in line, a man in front of us turned around and asked, "Are you Caleb Kaltenbach?" Now, I've been on staff at two churches in the Los Angeles area. I've also preached at several churches and spoken at conferences, events, and gatherings in Southern California. I tell you this because it's not unheard of for me to run into people at Disneyland who have heard one of my messages.

"You wrote *Messy Grace,* right?" he continued.

"Yeah," I said, trying to play it cool even though I was a little surprised.

"How did you recognize me?" I asked.

"I read your book! It was so helpful for me and other people in our church."

"Bro," I started, "thank you so much for sharing that with me. Now, tell me *your* story."

I listened as Brian Buxton told me about growing up in San

Diego in a Christian household with conservative views. As a kid, he was more into the arts than he was into playing sports. As a result, he was made fun of on a regular basis, even by his own family. He went to a Christian college and consistently prayed for God to take his attraction to men away, but it never happened. As time went on, he found himself struggling more and more.

In a blog post, Brian wrote the following about his struggle: "I looked and acted like a Christian to the whole world. While I don't doubt my resolve and commitment to the gospel of Christ, I see that my early upbringing in the church had influenced me to grow up and become a good legalist, not a faithful follower of Christ."[1]

Later, Brian heard a message preached by a pastor named J. D. Greear that changed his life. It helped him understand that a decision to be celibate does not earn God's love. Rather, Brian came to believe that the overflow of God's love for him is his motivation to follow Jesus as closely as he can in all areas of his life. Describing how Greear's message impacted him, Brian wrote that because of God's love, "I have the power to live my life, not obeying the temptations in my life."[2]

Brian is still a friend today. He's someone who has impeccable character, meaning that he lives out what he believes. More than most, he's careful that his theology, values, and decisions all align. Brian is a constant reminder to me that character is paramount, especially when I decide to journey with someone who is pursuing Jesus. If my integrity isn't solid, then eventually I'm not just sabotaging myself, but I'm hurting others and possibly even their views of Jesus. Also, there's a character problem when a redemptive community isn't living out their theological beliefs through what they say and how they treat others.

CHARACTER COUNTS

Your values—what's most important to you—serve as filters for the decisions you make. For instance, what if you get a job offer with a higher salary but it's in another state? Who doesn't need more money? However, what if moving your family isn't the best idea for your kids and spouse? What do you do? Your answer should already be determined by your values. If you value your family's well-being more than your career, then you have your answer. If it's the other way around, that's your answer. What if you are single and have been offered a higher-paying job in another state but the thought of leaving your family and friends is overwhelming? Again, depending on whom or what you value, your decision has already been made. You demonstrate basic character when your decisions are consistent with your values. Whether your character is good or bad depends on your values.

Some of my favorite definitions of *character* and/or *integrity* are

- "the ability to meet the demands of reality"[3]
- "the will to do what is right, as defined by God, regardless of personal cost"[4]
- "do[ing] the right thing, even if it's hard"[5]

Even though fewer and fewer people seem to possess character that is consistent with their decisions, I think most would agree that good character is a necessary attribute for humanity. However, in a world where it's assumed that Christians, politicians, and well-known celebrities don't have good character, it's an attractor when someone does. In his book *Louder Than Words,* pastor and author Andy Stanley stated, "Biblical character finds its source in the nature of our Creator rather than in the behavioral patterns of man. Good character is nothing less than a reflection of the character of God."[6] Our character should be a reflection of God's perfect character. Good character helps us walk with others and guide them closer to Jesus.

What if you want to walk with someone who is interested in following Jesus but has intimate relationships outside marriage? What if someone is still trying to decide what to do in response to their sexuality and asks you to journey with them? What if you were a church leader in my opening story in chapter 1 and the two couples asked you to advise them? Should you? Depending on the current state of your character, your decision has already been made. I hope you will measure your character before embarking on a spiritual journey with anyone. Ask yourself, *Do I have the credibility to walk with_____?*

> Our struggle, whatever it might be, can be powerful because it implies that we are striving toward God. It demonstrates that we still have faith.

I'm not insinuating that you should be perfect or without struggles. As a matter of fact, it's the struggle that makes us stronger—if we persevere. Our struggle, whatever it might be, can be powerful because it implies that we are striving toward God. It demonstrates that we still have faith.

Helen Keller once said, "Character cannot be developed in ease and quiet. Only through experience of trial and suffering can the soul be strengthened, vision cleared, ambition inspired, and success achieved."[7] Character is best sharpened in community with others. No one grows closer to Christ on their own. We all need each other as we walk through life.

I believe it's healthy to ask yourself on a regular basis if you do have the credibility to walk with someone. It might be helpful to reflect on these questions as well:

- Do you agree that what the person perceives to be a struggle is indeed a struggle?
- Are you greatly struggling with something similar to their struggle?
- Have you recently overcome a similar struggle? If so, will this journey hurt you?
- Are you making sinful decisions that will affect their journey in a negative way?
- Do you treat people well when they have this particular struggle?
- How do you expect to go about walking with them?
- What's your plan to make time in your schedule to walk with them?

Specifically, if someone who relates or identifies as LGBTQ asks you to walk with them, you need to examine your life. Throughout history, there have been many Christians who were critics of LGBTQ individuals even though they themselves were engaging in sex outside the theological guardrails they professed. The wake of bad character leaves behind a slew of spiritual chaos, hurt lives, and unnecessary doubts. Bad character wounds people.

If your character (or lack thereof) will be an obstacle to your journey with the individual, you may want to reconsider your plans. You *will* eventually be found out. As my friend Dusty Frizzell has said, "Character leaks."[8] Eventually, people see the *real you.*

If there are significant issues with your character, commit to the hard work of becoming emotionally and spiritually healthy before attempting to lead someone spiritually. Think of it this way—part of the way we love others well is by managing and growing our character. Again, I'm not advising you to be perfect. Everyone has issues and flaws; all of us are works in progress. Yet there's a tremendous difference between the character of someone who isn't perfect but strives to grow and someone with significant character issues that they refuse to deal with.

If the latter describes you, consider reflecting on these questions:

- Should you have a different strategy?
- Would it be better if someone else engaged?
- Is it wise to stay in the background for now?
- Could you recommend someone else?
- Can you remain a guide and faithful prayer warrior?

As political activist Thomas Paine said, "Character is much easier kept than recovered."[9] People watch the life you live and the decisions you make before they listen to whatever you say. In *Crucial Conversations,* author Kerry Patterson wrote, "As much as others may need to change, or we may *want* them to change, the only person we can continually inspire, prod, and shape—with any degree of success—is the person in the mirror."[10] Have you looked in the mirror yet? Let's continue diving into what it takes to measure character, as too often we cannot see our blind spots by ourselves.

SPIRITUALLY UNAWARE

Inattentional blindness occurs when we don't notice something or someone right in front of us because our focus is elsewhere. It's different from intentional blindness. My children consistently display intentional blindness. Case in point: more times than I can count, unseen tornadoes apparently sweep through my kids' rooms. Being a responsible parent, I ask them to clean their rooms. After one of my children claims to be finished cleaning their room, I bring their attention to a toy lightsaber or book on the floor. Then, in exaggerated bewilderment, my beloved child exclaims, "Oh, I didn't see *that*."

Okay, maybe this isn't *exactly* intentional blindness, but you get the idea.

As you well know, attention helps us perceive and notice details, situations, and people. Without it, no one could plan, use logic, or recall memories.[11] Unfortunately, inattentional blindness has caused major car accidents, crippled businesses, and so on, even into our spiritual lives.

I believe there's such a thing as *spiritual* inattentional blindness. It's experienced in different ways, one of which is taking sides between grace and truth. Those on the grace side can be blind to the depth of Scripture, and those siding with only truth seem unaware of how they treat people. One could even say that extremism and pride are by-products of spiritual inattentional blindness. A person who isn't developing their character, seeking to understand people, or deepening their relationship with Jesus is probably experiencing spiritual inattentional blindness. Such individuals are quick to recognize the flaws and faults of others while being unaware of their own sins.

Before Jesus's ministry, he was tempted in the desert for forty days and forty nights. Each temptation would have allowed Jesus to sidestep the Cross. In other words, Satan was saying, *Jesus, you don't have to go to this extreme. I can fast-track what you desire and with less pain.* It's an attractive offer! However, temptation never keeps its promises.

Though Jesus allowed himself to be tempted, he overcame and proved his credibility to move forward in his mission. I'm not recommending that you intentionally tempt yourself to see if you have what it takes. (Life offers us enough temptations.) I'd prefer you take Jesus's experience in the desert as motivation to look in the mirror and see if you have the character to walk with someone.

Pastor and author Paul David Tripp posed a good question to ask while gazing in the mirror: "Are there thoughts, motives, or attitudes (self-righteousness, anger, bitterness, spirit of condemnation, vengeance) that would get in the way of what God intends to do?"[12] Asking this question or brainstorming similar ones can help us realize what's going well in our lives, where we need growth, what might be out of place in our lives, or if there's anything in our lives that's confusing us or others. The stronger our faith and character, the more likely we are to help people and be an encouragement to them.

HOW YOU TREAT PEOPLE IS PART OF YOUR CHARACTER

Your character isn't only about keeping your word or maintaining consistency. If you are meeting the demands of reality and doing what's right, then loving and treating people well (what God says you must do) is a significant component of your character. Anyone who chooses not to be empathetic and who operates by assumptions isn't loving God and loving people. Such individuals have constructed an imaginary world where they reside and are easily able to meet the demands of their reality.

If you want to know the maturity of someone's character, then pay attention to how they treat others. Notice how and what they write on social media. Watch how they act toward anyone who lashes out at them. Just as the misalignment of our decisions and values compromises character, the contradiction of our values and treatment of others jeopardizes it.

> Just as the misalignment of our decisions and values compromises character, the contradiction of our values and treatment of others jeopardizes it.

At one time, Rosaria Butterfield (whom I mentioned in a previous chapter) was a professor at Syracuse University and in a relationship with another woman. She eventually trusted Jesus, left her romantic relationship, fell in love with and married a man, and became a mother. Currently, she's an author (a fantastic one at that) and speaker. Rosaria has been invited to numerous events, churches, groups, interviews, schools, colleges, and seminaries to share her testimony and perspective. At some of these gatherings, there were even demonstrations.

I admire Rosaria's uncanny possession of both fortitude and humility. In some instances, she heard about demonstrations beforehand and graciously asked for an open dialogue with individuals who held differing views from hers. I know she isn't perfect, but she seems like someone who tries hard to make few negative assumptions about others.

Here are five questions to ask yourself about character.

1. How Can I Be a Friend of Many Talents?

More than likely, when individuals relate or identify as LGBTQ, their relation or identification is not mainly about sex. Introducing them to Jesus and his reframing of their identity takes time, so give them the same margin you'd want others to give you. Remember the ultimate goal: influence. You earn the most influence by making relational investments instead of engaging in ridiculous arguments. Durable and faithful friendships are traveled on two-way streets. Deep and honest friendships will always result in more influence than shallow and simplistic relationships will.

Pastor and author Scott Sauls offered a way to tell the difference between one-dimensional and multifaceted relationships: "Friendships are one-dimensional when they revolve around a single shared interest and not much else. . . . One-dimensional friendships prioritize *sameness,* so views and convictions and practices are never challenged and blind spots are never uncovered. Friendships like these can't offer the natural, redemptive, character-forming tension that diversity brings to our lives."[13]

Here's what it boils down to: be a multifaceted friend. Endeavor to be a friend who asks tough questions, knows when to encourage and when to listen, understands how to communicate with others and what it takes to serve others, and works on being healthy in all areas of life. Being a multifaceted friend is far from a walk in the park, but our relationships should never be only about our needs. Usually, our healthiest relationships are the ones in which we attempt to serve others first as part of our worship of God.

The apostle Paul is a great example of the healthy side of relationships. He was willing to be intentional and meet people where they were instead of expecting them to meet him where he was. That intentional relational mindset was rare back in the first century and still is today. Simply scanning Paul's New Testament letters proves that he possessed a wealth of knowledge about societies, studied philosophical arguments of the Stoics and Epicureans, was a Roman citizen and an expert in the Old Covenant, made tents, seemed to keep current on sports, and liked being around people. Why was Paul versed in such a diversity of cultural knowledge?

Though Paul was passionate about learning, he cared even more for people. He was intentional about finding common ground with anyone, as he wrote to the Corinthians: "Though I am free and belong to no one, I have made myself a slave to everyone, to win as many as possible. . . . I have become all things to all people so that by all possible means I might save some. I do all this for the sake of the gospel, that I may share in its blessings" (1 Corinthians 9:19, 22–23). The degree Paul would go to for the sake of a relationship was truly extraordinary.

> We tend to make better decisions when the right people surround us.

Tyler Chernesky is a pastor and good friend of mine. If Tyler becomes your friend, then you've gained someone who genuinely wants to help make your life better. Tyler has learned a significant lesson that I'm still learning: we tend to make better decisions when the right people surround us. He's surrounded himself with a strong community of friends and family. Though he experiences loneliness in the midst of his celibacy, he's thought deeply about what being a good friend entails. In one of his blog posts, he wrote, "Good friends take the time to explore their own hearts. They assess their motives and desires and honestly evaluate what makes them tick. They name old wounds and identify the effects of those wounds."[14]

2. How Do Others Feel Around Me?

How do others—especially LGBTQ individuals—feel around you? My friend Jeff wisely asks himself, *What is it like to be on the other side of me?* What is your attitude toward others? How do people perceive your attitude? Do individuals feel comfortable around you? Why or why not? Jesus believed that how others felt around him mattered, and he was an expert at getting the right kind of emotion from people. Andy Stanley's description of how Jesus impacted people is perfect:

> People who were nothing like him liked him. And Jesus liked people who were nothing like him. Jesus invited unbelieving, misbehaving, troublemaking men and women to follow him and to embrace something new, and they accepted his invitation.
>
> As followers of Jesus, we should be known as people who like people who are nothing like us.[15]

If people who were nothing like Jesus liked him, is this still true today? When it comes to discussions on ethics, values, theology, or tough conversations, out of all the first-century leaders, we need to start with Jesus. Maybe others will like us more if we're more like Jesus. Of course, getting people to "like" us isn't the goal we're discussing here. Being able to foster meaningful and multifaceted friendships depends on how people feel around you.

3. Do I Need to Own a Sin?

What about all the sins you willfully commit? Has anyone noticed your less-than-sly attempts to cover up your hypocrisy? Do you hide behind the name *Christian* or use grace as a credit card? Want to talk about the gossip you shared? When was the last time you exaggerated words so you'd appear better? Is that one website you visited really a secret? I guess as long as you've cleared the search history, it never happened, right? Did you enjoy your inappropriately long conversation you had with that certain individual who isn't your spouse? How's your language? When are you actually *not* on an electronic device? What's your pride telling you to do these days? Have you dealt with the last anger outburst you had toward your kids? When will you say that enough is enough with how much you eat?

Everyone has struggles and weaknesses, but there's a difference between the believer who is willing to look in the mirror and the believer who is not. Dealing with the struggles of others starts by addressing the problems in ourselves. We are only as strong as the last sin we surrendered to God. And trust me, it's safe to surrender to him. God longs for surrendered leaders, not perfect ones.

People can see the contrast between a Christian who makes repentance a spiritual discipline and one who merely makes excuses. Each time we look in the mirror and repent makes us more gracious, compassionate, honest, and forgiving.

4. Is There Someone I Need to Forgive or Reconcile With?

What's getting in the way of you loving others? Is there someone you need to forgive? Maybe someone who relates as LGBTQ hurt you and really affected your view of other LGBTQ individuals. Perhaps a Christian hurt a friend who is gay or lesbian and it has affected your view of the Christians you consider too conservative. My buddy, pastor Rusty George, has a way of making statements that are simultaneously convicting and encouraging. I love this statement he's made: "It can be exhausting to always be reminding yourself who you are mad at and why. Letting that burden go can be life-giving to you as well."[16]

Whatever bitterness might be holding back your forgiveness, you'll never let go of it until Jesus is and remains your primary focal point. Pastor and author Timothy Keller made this point well when he said, "Unless I see that Jesus made the big sacrifices *for* me, I will never be able to make the normal sacrifices in life. Unless I can see him as forgiving *me* on the cross, I won't be able to forgive others."[17]

I cannot count the number of times I've sat down with parents who have not spoken to their adult children for years because their child came out to them and they saw their dreams for their kids shattered. Likewise, I've spoken with many young people who refuse contact with their parents or other family members because they didn't agree with their decision to be in a relationship with someone of the same sex. As we covered in a previous chapter, acceptance (loving people no matter what) and agreement (with a choice, opinion, or relationship decision) are *not* the same thing.

Sadly, when our emotions control us, the future's uncertainty overwhelms us. Emotions cloud clarity.

5. Who Does Jesus Compel Me to Be?

Pose this question when you're measuring your character for the sake of relationships. Should you create room in your life for people who relate or identify as LGBTQ? What did Jesus do in similar situations? Who did he surround himself with? In other words, *Who does Jesus compel me to be?* Instead of attacking those who hurt you, ask, *Who does Jesus compel me to be?* When you experience vagueness over identity or feel inclined to shift your beliefs to eliminate the tension of grace and truth, ask, *Who does Jesus compel me to be?*

Who does Jesus compel you to be? An influencer. Remember, influence is gained by making consistent relational investments in people. Investing means being fully present with people, helping them, listening to them, lovingly telling them the truth, keeping your word, treating them well, and serving as an example for them. Text messages, little acts of service, looking someone in the eye, and writing a note matter more than you know. Such seemingly insignificant gestures are significant to others because they help them see you as consistent and loving.

Good character and earned influence compel people to tell good stories about you. The same is true about the character and influence of your church, small group, gathering of friends, and so on. When telling stories, people frame them within their perspectives (their feelings, opinions, and experience). Just as trust is hard to rebuild, perspective is difficult to reframe. But when people tell good stories about churches and the Christian community, it makes it easier for others to believe in Jesus.

PRIORITIZING AND PREPARING
FOR DIALOGUE

Michael was sobbing in my office. He had asked to meet with me just a few minutes before our church's young-adult worship service began. I was the young-adult pastor at a church in Los Angeles, and Michael had moved to LA to attend college. He was quieter than the other students, so when he asked to meet with me, I was thrilled for the chance to get to know him better. However, I had no idea our first talk would be like this.

His tears had already stained his face and made his eyes appear bloodshot. I came from around the desk and sat next to him.

"What's going on, bro?" I asked with my hand on his shoulder.

No reply—just more crying. I began to assume that one of his friends died recently or a parent had cancer or something. Thankfully, I wasn't preaching that day, because it was now fifteen minutes or so into the worship service. I consider myself compassionate, but it was time for him to start spilling his guts.

"Michael, tell me what happened. Why are you so upset?"

He removed his face from his hands, looked at me, and said, "I'm a sinner and my parents hate me!"

"Huh?" I replied. "We're all sinners. Why would your parents hate you for that?"

He proceeded to tell me that he had come out to his very conservative Christian parents. Now everything was making more sense. I could already imagine how the conversation went down, and I was right. And to top it off, his parents didn't appreciate that he had his coming-out conversation with them over the phone instead of in person.

> "Empathy doesn't require that we have the exact same experiences as the person sharing their story with us."

Painful words and sentiments had been exchanged as their interaction became more intense. One phrase stuck with him that his parents intended to be comforting but Michael found insulting. These six words comprise a saying that I've come to despise: "Love the sinner, but hate the sin."

If there was ever a phrase I wish I could remove from the Western Christian subculture, it's this one. I think those six words have wrecked relationships, divided families, ensured lonely holidays, and brought depressed feelings more than anyone knows.

The phrase has too much baggage, so let's just lose it. Trust me: there are better approaches. If the conversation calls for it, we could instead say the following:

- "My beliefs about marriage, sex, and relationships don't affect how much I value and love you."
- "You and I have differing beliefs about relationships and sexuality, but I also believe that Jesus loves you no matter what—and I do too!"
- "I may not agree with every decision, opinion, or belief

that others hold—no one does—but I'll never stop accepting you or anyone else. A loving relationship is built on acceptance."

- "I love you no matter what, and our disagreement doesn't cause me to stop loving you."

- "Yeah, I have my beliefs about many things, but you know what I believe about you? I believe God created you and Jesus died for you, so I will never stop valuing you or start to treat you differently."

God deserves to be better represented by what we say.

Today a growing number of people believe that others cannot relate with them unless they've had identical experiences. While this idea has some merits, it also contains major problems. Though experiences may be comparable, no two people can have the same exact experience. Related circumstances (that might be almost identical) can bring differing experiences. Past and present situations, upbringing, biological factors, joys, pains, and more cause us to perceive events differently. Additionally, though there might be similarities, each of us processes experiences differently in our minds. Quite a bit of our interpretations of our experiences happen while we are alone and aren't shared with other people and, thus, cannot be completely understood by others.

Author Brené Brown said, "Empathy doesn't require that we have the exact same experiences as the person sharing their story with us."[1] As we learned in an earlier chapter, we can connect with others on emotional levels. Not everyone can understand your experiences, but they can still relate and empathize with you. And as we learn how to relate and empathize with people, our conversations—even the difficult ones—will become healthier. We'll get better at handling conversations about following Jesus and living for him. And Christians need to get better at conversations, because there have been centuries upon centuries of God's people not permeating difficult conversations with grace and truth.

PREPARE FOR THE CONVERSATION

While conversations about following Jesus well are always difficult, the emotions in the discussion immediately rise to another level of complexity when sexuality is addressed. Some conversations might be difficult, but they never have to destroy. Prioritizing and preparing will help you be intentional with your words.

The worst thing you can do in a conversation is react instead of respond. A *reaction* is usually impulsive, off the cuff, and said with little thought and no preparation. Differently, a *response* is intentional and planned and seeks the best for all involved.

In this chart, you can see some of the differences between the two words.

REACTION	RESPONSE
Sudden and impulsive	Intentionally planned
Spewing emotions	Managing emotions
Little or no prayer	Grounded in prayer and Scripture
Problem focused	Solution driven
Self-protecting	Caring for others
Long-term damage	Moving toward long-term care

The more you can plan and prepare, the more effective you'll be when you need to have challenging conversations. Here are seven tips for preparing for and engaging in tough discussions with intentionality.

1. Ask Yourself Questions First

We've discussed the importance of asking good questions, but I want to emphasize it again here. Before having a difficult conversation, you need to think through your approach and motivation. You especially need to look at what the Bible has to say about the situation and ask questions of the verses you read.

Some good questions to ask yourself might be:

- What do I hope to get out of the conversation?
- What is this person struggling with? What are they not struggling with?
- How should I bring up the conversation?
- What can I do to help them take one more step toward Jesus?
- How can I emphasize my love for them and God's love for them?

Without preparation, your discussion will be sideways energy (in other words, leading both of you nowhere other than to frustration).

2. Determine the Goal of the Conversation

In tense dialogues, regardless of how gracious you try to be, people will hear what they want to hear and how they want to hear it. Everyone has filters they use when uncomfortable, especially when a person feels they must go on the defensive. One way to help the conversation rise above such actions is to determine the goal of the conversation.

As a Christian psychologist who has had his share of difficult conversations, Dr. Mark Yarhouse wrote the following about goals in conversations and dialogue: "We must have people think about who they are in terms that go beyond their same-sex sexuality—looking to a broader sense of identity and what their sexuality means to them in light of their faith."[2]

When you have to tell someone the truth about how they are or are not following Jesus, never forget that the ultimate goal is to help that person take another step toward Jesus, whatever that next step looks like.

It's also helpful to remember that the goal is *not*

- having them praise your logic in the conversation
- demonstrating better argumentation skills
- manipulating emotionally
- venting

The goal isn't to encourage ego-driven morality. Behavior modification for the sake of behavior modification is so far away from a Christ-centered goal that it will make you look like a Pharisee. If behavior modification itself is the goal, then guilt will be your main tool to convince the individual and shame will probably overtake them. Guilt-driven obligation breeds nothing but resentment toward you and, worse yet, God.

If the conversation becomes about a win for yourself, then you've already trashed your influence. You probably aren't interested in investing in the other person as much as competing with that individual. Don't turn a grace-and-truth discussion into an argument. Taking advantage of your influence to win an argument is a sure way to lose a relationship.

> Be more interested in maintaining influence for the long haul.

This probably goes without saying, but the ultimate goal is life change through Jesus. Your priority is to help people identify with Jesus and follow him well. You aren't here to win a debate. While I absolutely believe that orthodox theology is a nonnegotiable, I don't have conversations to show everyone how correct I am. Rather, sound doctrine helps me empathetically direct people to Jesus.

Your friendships are marathons, not sprints. Be more interested in maintaining influence for the long haul than in experiencing the prideful short-term satisfaction of flexing your theological biceps.

3. Emphasize Jesus's Love for That Person

If devotion to Christ above all else is the goal, lives will eventually change. Personally, I want people to know how much Jesus loves them. When people start to believe how much Jesus loves them and they love him back, devotion to him starts to develop.

Now, if we follow Jesus, are we obligated to structure our lives around his words? Yes! But as author Jackie Hill Perry described, when devotion precedes obligation, people grow in more spiritually healthy ways:

> I know now what I didn't know then. God was not calling me to be straight; He was calling me to Himself. The choice to lay aside sin and take hold of holiness was not synonymous with heterosexuality. . . . In my becoming Holy as He is, I would not be miraculously made into a woman that didn't like women; I'd be made into a woman that loved God more than anything.[3]

Devotion to Jesus is better than following him out of obligation. After all, wasn't God devoted to pursuing you before you understood the rules? Didn't he chase after you when you didn't even give him much thought? Doesn't he still hold on to the relationship even when you are going through a season of not being as close to him? Shouldn't you do the same for others? Obligation without relationship breeds resentment, but devotion allows love.

Love is the ultimate application of every theological idea found in the Bible. It's important to keep love in mind as we prepare to discuss theological aspects in the conversation, because an individual's perspective on an issue is rarely aligned with ours.

4. Realize Possible Differentiation of Perspectives

Reality becomes messy anytime our beliefs collide with contrasting opinions. It's easier to manufacture villains out of those who disagree with me than learn more about them and invite them to dialogue. Without dialogue, Jesus followers will never become bridges for society. Little headway will be made if we assume the worst about affirming *and* nonaffirming people.

In recent years, I've noticed a trend: Christians maintain an overarching belief about major societal issues, but depending on context and life domain, they have different perspectives or applications of those issues. To say it a different way, a person might have a core belief about a topic but have different perspectives on that topic (ethical, civil, or theological). While there are times that differing perspectives on an issue might be positive or negative, it's a way of life. Just as you can experience various emotions about an individual, you can have different perspectives on an issue.

For instance, one person believes God originally created marriage to be between a man and woman (she might add more detail in her theological perspective). At the same time, since the Supreme Court's ruling on *Obergefell v. Hodges* (marriage equality) in 2015, her civil view is that people should have the right to marry someone of the same sex because it's the law. Another person might be pro-life. Theologically, he believes that life occurs at conception and should be protected. Ethically, he struggles with whether or not abortion should be allowed in some medical situations. Civilly, he doesn't think tax dollars should fund abortions but struggles with the legality of a complete abortion ban (given there might be some unique medical scenarios). He also realizes how some individuals view him as a hypocrite because he believes all life is sacred but supports the death penalty.

People have had experiences and studied concepts that have led them to the beliefs and opinions they currently hold. Whether you agree with someone or not, use caution in how you treat them and what you say to them. As we'll discuss soon, it's important to disagree in healthy ways and harmful to do otherwise. With those ideas in mind, let's discuss how to be intentional in planning difficult conversations.

5. Plan Out Empathetic Conversations

People aren't going to like what you have to say, so ask yourself questions about what direction you want the conversation to go. While there's an ultimate goal for each truth conversation, you may have a goal for that person or next steps that are unique to your conversation. What do you want the person to do after the conversation? How do you want them to respond? Those are two very important questions to ask yourself as you move forward. Where do you see a misalignment in their life with Jesus, and how can you best help them own this misalignment? What is the best-case scenario at the end of the conversation?

Good intentions don't always result in ideal outcomes. I've found that if you're having a difficult conversation, you're probably going to have more than one. It's impossible to show empathy or say what needs to be said in a single discussion about a personal aspect of an individual's life. Harriet Beecher Stowe's words seem appropriate: "The bitterest tears shed over graves are for words left unsaid and deeds left undone."[4] Preparation can be all the difference between a conversation that goes well and one that could have gone well, between words that could've been said and words that were said. Too many interactions flop for a lack of preparation.

Have a planned beginning and end to the conversation. Stick to one subject and try not to let the discussion become the never-ending talk. The longer the conversation is, the more emotionally charged it becomes and the further away the conversation moves from its purpose. To avoid such a distraction, know what you want to say and how you want to say it. Let me be even more specific: *write down what you're going to say.* Think in terms of how you need to structure your part of the conversation. Also, if the person is open to scheduling the conversation, consider a location where they will best hear your words. What setting will be most appealing to them? If the conversation could be emotional, what time of day would be most appropriate? Would it be a good idea to meet in public?

Perhaps most important, you need to imagine potential responses by being empathetic. You need to put yourself in the other person's shoes. If you don't, there's a high probability the conversation will go south. Think about the talk from the other person's perspective because, as Dr. Henry Cloud and Dr. John Townsend wrote, "You don't see things the same way nor feel the same way, and you have different ideas on what to do about it. This is not a bad thing, in and of itself."[5]

Naturally, the person you're sharing with may feel attacked. God's truth stands in opposition to the insecurities of people or whatever has dominated them. In a way, truth can trigger painful emotions much like alcohol on an open wound.

6. Find the Right Time

When and *how* you say something is often as important as *what* you say. Wait for the right opportunity, and don't force the conversation. This might sound cliché, but wait on God's timing.

Often he takes the conversation in certain directions. Mark Moore, one of my college professors, was well known for saying, "The Holy Spirit does what he wants, when he wants, and how he wants" (see 1 Corinthians 12:11). While our longing for supernatural divine inspiration in that moment is valid, it should never be used as an excuse to not prepare. If God does direct the conversation in another way, trust him to give you the words to say.

Also, trust God even if the discussion seems to come out of nowhere. Do you ever notice how needed conversations just happen? "We live in a world where spontaneous and informal conversations—with their lack of agreed upon rules and goals— bombard us. In short, we should aspire to a world of dialogue but may live in a world of conversation."[6] I'm sure that at one time or another, you've had difficult conversations spring up on you. During these unexpected times, listen for the person to make statements or ask questions, such as:

- "I broke up with the person I've been dating."
- "I'm not sure if this relationship is right for me."
- "What do you think about faith and _____?"
- "I can't move on from my significant other."
- "I'm a moron (or insert any other self-derogatory reference)."
- "No one understands me or even tries to. No one listens to me."
- "I feel alone."
- "I've tried praying, but nothing happens."
- "God isn't helping me."

These are all catalysts for you to share about your faith and hope and how identifying with Jesus means you're with the One who knows you the best and still loves you the most.

Even though impromptu conversations pop up, try not to talk when you're tired. Usually, late at night isn't ideal. It might be best to schedule the conversation for the next day or another time if your emotions are worn out, if the other person has a lot going on, when either of you are stressed, or if you're around a lot of people.

7. Practice and Pray

Craft solution-oriented questions for the conversation. Also, you can use a technique called funneling, whereby you ask general questions and then make the follow-up questions more and more specific. Write down your questions, memorize them, and have spare ones at the ready. Realize that conversations can and often do have spontaneous direction. Thus, you shouldn't be married to all your questions, but be ready to try to redirect the conversation.

If the person means a lot to you, they deserve nothing less than your best. Your intentionality and commitment to excellence are required, so practice, practice, and practice again. Rehearse your part of the conversation out loud and go over it in your head. Repeatedly ask God what he wants you to say or not say.

> Since prayer is your direct connection to God, your love for a person only increases when you consistently pray for that person.

In other words, as you plan, listen, and practice, you'll want to *pray.* Pray again. Then pray some more. The more you pray, the better prepared you are.

Not to get into a theological debate, but I don't believe that prayer changes God's mind. Personally, I'm convinced that he has complete knowledge of what was, is, will be, and could have been. Faith isn't increased by changing his mind but by drawing close to him. Since prayer is your direct connection to God, your love for a person only increases when you consistently pray for that person. Just as God is your Father, he is that individual's Father too. When you pray, your heart becomes more aligned with God. Inevitably, you will love that individual more as you draw closer to the One who loves them the most.

Intentionality in praying, planning, and trusting God all communicate how much you value the person you're speaking to. People are more likely to value your words if they feel like you care.

DIFFICULT CONVERSATIONS
THAT DON'T DESTROY

I t's tough to relax when a difficult conversation is looming on
your horizon. Just thinking about it can ignite anxiety, discomfort, stress, anger, bitterness, or sadness. If you're like me, you
might even have physical reactions such as stomach pains and
headaches. Those physical feelings should serve as reminders for
us to draw closer to God. He may not remove the emotional
weight of the upcoming conversation (because loving others well
is difficult), but he can give us peace. If God removed the burden
of a tough conversation, he'd be eliminating love from the situation, and love requires sacrifice. Love means that we carry burdens into difficult scenarios. Our love for someone may force us
to carry those burdens with us for a while, but God will get us
through it. He never speaks to us through worry, bitterness, ha-
tred, envy, confusion, and the like; those tools belong to the
Enemy. As a result, people usually attempt to resolve their unset-
tled feelings with unhealthy methods such as ignoring the need to
meet, finding reasons not to meet, or putting off the meeting.

Perhaps you're someone who delays needed discussions. Maybe

you reason that in one way or another, the issues will be resolved. For you, the price of not having difficult conversations seems less than having them. You could be hoping that any negative feelings will just fade away. (Spoiler: emotions rarely, if at all, work like that.) Maybe you act in passive-aggressive ways toward the person you're having the conversation with. It may be that you didn't prepare well for the discourse and begin to treat the person you'll be speaking with indifferently. There might have been times when you wanted to rush into an uneasy discussion but did so with little prayer and hardly any empathy. Chances are the individual walked away from the conversation and didn't make spiritually healthy decisions. As a result, your influence was shattered.

> Not preparing, rushing to talk, ignoring our loved ones, or treating them harshly are some of the most un-Christlike things we could do.

Without intentional planning and self-control in the moment, we're going to communicate God's words in unhelpful ways and potentially harm someone we care about. If we rush to have the conversation without deep prayer, an intentional plan, or empathy, we won't inspire the person toward Jesus. Not preparing, rushing to talk, ignoring our loved ones, or treating them harshly are some of the most un-Christlike things we could do. The people we value need better. Our relationships deserve better. Jesus is worthy of better.

CONVERSATION FAIL

"Do you even realize how you've made me feel?" That's what Connor said to me as he looked at me in disbelief. A couple of weeks earlier, he had contacted me to set up a meeting. For a few months, he had been attending the church I was leading in Dallas but had some questions. Throughout the previous few years, he had been in and out of churches that were loving but were mostly non-affirming of same-sex relationships.

I had come to know Connor through my conversations in between Sunday-morning services. You know those conversations, right? The ones in which you lie to the pastor with accolades: "It can't get any better than that!" or "I'm sure going to remember that message!"

Connor would approach and ask questions about the message, share an idea he heard in a sermon on a podcast the previous week, or request prayer for the next few days. After a few weeks of these conversations, he sat in my office and asked, "What do you believe God says about homosexuality? I'm gay and I need to know."

I had an idea of what he was going to ask, but I didn't pray or prepare well. It had been a busy week. Even to this day, I remember how busy that week was, but I mostly remember how awful I made Connor feel.

Not thinking deeply enough, I started rattling off Bible verses like a commentary written by a nineteenth-century theologian who was dead.

Connor motioned with his hand for me to stop and said, "I know all those verses."

There was a brief silence in the room as I just stared at him. However, I began to hear a little voice in my head telling me, *You are acting like a moron!*

"I asked what you believe God says about homosexuality," Connor clarified.

"I told you what I believe," I responded.

The little voice in my head was a bit louder now: *Redirect the conversation!*

Unfortunately, I didn't listen to the voice and said, "I believe what the Bible says."

Here's a free tip: when you have to make a general statement like "I believe what the Bible says" without specifying the verses and passages, then you're in trouble. You've thrown down the trump card and automatically implied that you're correct and the other person is wrong. How do you think an absolute statement makes others feel?

Hear me out: I do believe what the Bible says and deem it to be true, but in that moment, I hadn't slowed my thinking down enough or been intentional enough to realize what Connor was asking. In so many words, he was asking me, "What does God think about me?" Looking back, the unspoken deeper question Connor posed was, "If I'm gay, does God love me?"

The voice in my head was now in bullhorn mode: *Admit that you're a moron and apologize!*

Silence.

Apologize!!! the voice cried out again.

But I still sat there in silence, not knowing what to do. That's when Connor got up and said, "Do you even realize how you've made me feel?"

Connor left the office shortly after that. Despite my efforts to contact him and apologize, I haven't seen him since.

So, what did I do wrong? Oh, let's count the many errors!

- I didn't pray or plan.
- I didn't think more deeply about him.
- I disrespected him.
- I shared Bible verses as though I were reading a cue card.
- I didn't listen to my gut.

And the list could go on. But those are examples of what not to do when you're in a difficult conversation about grace and truth. Let's imagine for a moment that you are presently in such a conversation. What next? Now that you're in the thick of it, how do you proceed?

WHEN YOU'RE IN THE CONVERSATION

We were created for relationship with others, and God himself serves as an example of community. Besides your thoughts, the bulk of your life is experienced within the social context of relationships. There's an innate sense in all of us that feels a responsibility to take care of the earth and each other. It's difficult to steward this world and our relationships when society has a gravitational pull away from God. Loving and serving people not only helps them but also enriches the ones doing the helping.

In that light, conversations about following Jesus and sexuality are difficult, but such discussions don't have to destroy others.

In the pages to come, I want to offer some tips that will guide us in having tough conversations in love without hurting anyone. Whereas in the previous chapter I shared seven ways to prepare for dialogue, here are seven ideas to keep in mind for when you're actually involved in the conversation.

1. Be Fully Present

Sometimes, being fully present with someone means being physically present with that individual. While empathy doesn't offer a silver-bullet solution, it can be a catalyst to unify us. When we acknowledge people and are fully present with them, we'll discover things we have in common (life experiences, movie preferences, concerns, frustrations). Acknowledgment begins with getting to know someone despite the opinions of others.

Are you willing to be misunderstood by your peers so you can be *with* others? Paul was willing. Jesus certainly was (see Matthew 9:9–13). I don't think Jesus ever paced back and forth pondering, *I wonder what others will think. Will Caiaphas be okay with my decision to ask a tax collector to join me? What will my cousin John say to others about how I let Mary follow me?*

Jesus never had anxiety over his peers' approval, yet when he stood with people, he never justified their sin. Paul and Jesus were more concerned about doing what was right and being with others.

2. Talk Less So You Can Listen More

When people feel listened to and validated and are asked questions that get their minds processing, they feel safe. When people feel safe, they are more likely to share their thoughts, feelings, and ideas.

If you think listening is easy, you probably don't do it well. My wife is a therapist and has told me time and time again how difficult it can be to *really* listen. It can drain your energy and leave your emotions feeling spent. My strategy while I listen intently to people is to have their story playing in my head as if it's a movie. Without knowing it, I start reacting on a very low level as if what happened to them (as portrayed in my head) is happening to me. This practice doesn't work for everyone, but it personally helps me listen more and talk less.

Listening well relies on consistent eye contact. There are times during the conversation when I'm tempted to look everywhere else but toward the person talking to me. Now, if you're ADHD like me, you also know that sometimes looking elsewhere can enhance listening, but the other person usually assumes that you are not interested in the conversation. Eye contact communicates a tremendous amount of value to the other person. Whether intended or not, a lack of eye contact communicates a lack of interest. Because I tend to be distracted, I bring a notepad and pen to take notes (if I have their permission). Afterward, I usually throw the notes away. The notepad and pen were merely tools to keep my attention (and the appearance of it) engaged.

Also, repeating what you hear the person say is important. When you're able to, say, "If I hear you correctly . . ." or "What I've heard you say so far is . . ." This summary should be no more than a couple of sentences. This technique of restating not only gives them a chance to correct you if you're off track but also validates them if they need empathy. When people feel heard by you, they tend to trust you more and more.

3. Show Respect

Henry Wasonga Abuto is a Christian who describes himself as gay and celibate. After participating in a roundtable with other LGBTQ individuals, Henry wrote the following on his blog:

> Understanding someone else's experiences allows you to see how they arrived where they are. Even if I don't agree with where someone lands, it costs me nothing to respect their experience, and it's an added benefit if I learn from it.[1]

Spot on. Disrespecting a person's experiences or views is a surefire way to quickly end the conversation. It's impossible to influence people if they feel disrespected. When we immediately dismiss their opinions, ideas, thoughts, views, and political stances without first listening to them, we'll never earn the respect needed to help them. As you start a difficult conversation with someone, keep this question in mind: "What point/perspective does this person bring to the table that I am blind to/have not considered?"[2]

Such a good question. During the conversation, stop acting like you understand everything. Quit acting like you get it. Just listen to people. Do more listening than sharing. Don't assume you know what someone is going through even if you think you have similar experiences. *You don't.* What happened to both of you may have been similar, but how you both processed it (or will process it) is more different than what you assume.

> Don't assume you know what someone is going through even if you think you have similar experiences. *You don't.*

4. Think About How You Can Encourage the Person

Ever had a situation in which you worked hard on a project and then presented it to others? At the end of the presentation, you received many compliments, but instead of remembering those accolades, you kept focusing on that one individual who had too many questions or one critical comment. Later that evening, you start having imaginary conversations in your head with that individual where you defend your hard work and tell them what you really think about their comments. We can probably all relate to this scenario. That's why we should focus on encouraging others more than on anything else.

I love how my friends Rusty George and Michael DeFazio have talked about encouraging others: "When Jesus tells us to let our light shine, it isn't to show people how blind they are or how bright we are but rather to show them the way to God."[3] Similarly, Dr. Henry Cloud has said that most people need five encouraging messages for each negative experience or conversation. According to Dr. Cloud, "The brain needs a lot of love, safety, and good feelings to be able to handle negative inputs and use them."[4] People respond well and are more open to listening to you when they're encouraged by you. Please understand that I'm not recommending gimmicks. I believe that you should encourage the real attributes they possess.

I know this to be true because I see it in my own children. Like most people, both of my kids are emotional; however, they show this emotion in different ways. Whereas my daughter doesn't hide her feelings well, my son can. He went through a rough season in elementary school in which he would internalize his feelings. Even though he wouldn't always respond emotionally like his sister, I could see the shame and negative talk in his head when they got in trouble. Eventually, I realized that when he did get in trouble (which was quite often in those days), I would need to strategically plan four or five compliments or kind messages and some video-game time. If I intentionally did those things, he'd bounce back more quickly. If I didn't, let's just say it would be a long day!

5. Share What You Believe to Be True

I still remember the first time I read these words written by pastor and author John Ortberg: "People who love authentic community always prefer the pain of temporary chaos to the peace of permanent superficiality. Telling people what they want to hear is not love."[5] I didn't like what he said at all. I mean, who likes pain? Who wants to hurt the people they love (even if it's temporary pain)? In time, I realized Ortberg was correct. I applaud what he wrote! I only wish more people lived as he was describing and cared enough about each other to have such conversations. Unfortunately, we do not, which is why we must engage in truth.

Eventually, you'll get to the point in which you need to share truth in some way. When this happens, be bold about sharing, but try your best not to be overly personal with the individual or attack them with words.

They may not appreciate your words. They might respond by saying, "I knew I shouldn't have trusted you," or, "You let me down." If they do make statements like those, it's best to let them talk. Just listen. If they want to fight, respond, but don't start a verbal shouting match. Ask them, "Could you help me understand how I've hurt you in the past?" Asking a question like this that points backward to your relationship is why it's vital to have measured your credibility to see if you have the character to engage.

Remember, if you have even a small feeling that your purpose for the conversation is for you to be correct, get rid of that feeling! Surrender your ego and embrace humility.

6. Allow Difference

The right message in the wrong tone has the wrong impact. Usually, people have trouble controlling their first reaction, but you can be intentional in how you respond after that first reaction. Darrell Bock and Mikel Del Rosario explained it like this: "A person is more likely to receive our critique when they know that we respect them, care to understand them, and ultimately have their best interests in mind. All this takes compassion and patience while working relationally with someone who may see Christianity differently than we do. This brings to mind the ethos of loving your neighbor as yourself."[6]

Manage your emotions as the conversation proceeds. The person you're talking to may say rude things to you. The individual probably won't agree or understand where you're coming from. You may walk away with hurt feelings. Even so, remain calm and assured. The calmer you are and the more you respect the other person while you share truth, the better the conversation will be. Remember, you're the one who has planned the conversation. You've chosen to respond instead of reacting in the moment. More than likely, the person you're speaking with is reacting out of their immediate feelings in the moment. Don't take what they say too personally and give them time to process everything after the meeting.

7. Reassure Them

Often, during and after a difficult truth conversation, people need to be reassured of their value to you or their value in the relationship. Too many people allow difficult conversations to end on a tough note and wonder why the next interactions with the other person are so awkward. This can be difficult to see if you're the one who is initiating the tough discussion. So, here are some suggestions and questions to reflect on before having the conversation.

Put yourself in the other person's shoes. What would you want said to you? As a tough conversation goes on, where would you want reassurance? Where might you feel the relationship is in jeopardy? If you were in their shoes, what would you think or assume after the conversation?

In addition to considering how they might feel leaving the conversation, we should reassure people of our love for them because God regularly reassures us of his love for us. Dr. Miroslav Volf boils it down for us: "Because there is one God, all people are related to that one God on equal terms. The central command of that one God is to love neighbors—to treat others as we would like them to treat us, as expressed in the Golden Rule."[7] It might be good to ask yourself, *If I were this person, how would I want to be treated? How would I want to feel after I leave the conversation?*

AFTER THE CONVERSATION

What do you do at the conversation's end? Maybe you tried to share your faith in Jesus, but your friend didn't jump off the chair and immediately become a Christian. There's a good chance that you tried to warn them about some decisions they made or a relationship. Whatever the case, rarely is there a resolution or repentance after one conversation. Resolutions and repentance usually take time.

Rosaria Butterfield wrote some winsome words on repentance:

> I learned the first rule of repentance: that repentance requires greater intimacy with God than with our sin. . . . Repentance requires that we draw near to Jesus, no matter what. And sometimes we all have to crawl there on our hands and knees. Repentance is an intimate affair. And for many of us, intimacy with anything is a terrifying prospect.[8]

I appreciate Rosaria's words: "Repentance requires greater intimacy with God than with our sin." We have to continually learn how to love God more than our sin, and that demands the reoccurring act of dying to self. It's why no one quickly deepens their relationship with God. More than likely, this is also why you discovered that when the difficult conversation was over, not everything went your way. Now you're trying to figure out what's next. This is a crucial time, because you don't want to walk away from the process you started or give up on the person you talked to.

There are a few intentional things you can do to keep you engaged in the process.

Keep Praying and Consider How You Will Reengage

As I said earlier, you're probably going to have more than one conversation, so don't be angry or disappointed that there wasn't resolution after this conversation or that you must have another conversation in your future. Difficult conversations are usually best when they have one main point to communicate plus time to process afterward. People need that time to process, to "look in the mirror." Tim Winters, the executive pastor at Shepherd Church (the church I attend) has often said, "We're emotionally attached to our destructive thoughts and toxic behaviors."

Sometimes it's challenging to let go of our destructive thoughts and habits because we've become accustomed to thinking and acting in those ways. This may sound cliché, but *trust God.* Timothy Keller said that when we pray, "God will either give us what we ask or give us what we would have asked if we knew everything he knew."[9] Whatever happens and whatever the outcome, God loves you, the person you're engaging, and everyone else involved in the situation.

Evaluate How the Conversation Went

Howard Hendricks is well known for saying, "Experience does not necessarily make you better; in fact it tends to make you worse, unless it's evaluated experience."[10] If you simply walk away from the conversation and don't evaluate yourself, you'll never grow from the experience. Refusing to evaluate how things went assures that any mistakes or assumptions from the first conversation will repeat themselves in the next conversation. Ultimately, this could very well derail the work God wants to do in you and in the other person.

Unintentional helpful evaluation rarely happens. So, intentionally set some time aside to evaluate your role in the conversation. Ask yourself (or someone else, if they were with you) these questions:

- How did I meet or not meet my goal?
- Where in the conversation, if at all, did the other person respond positively?
- Did I say what I needed to say?
- How well did I listen?
- Did I share graciously what I believe to be true?
- How did I encourage the person in other areas of their life?
- Did I encourage them enough or not enough?
- What was missing from the conversation?
- What could I have done better?
- Did I honor the person's time?
- How was the location?

When you meet again with the person you had the conversation with, ask them how they felt about the conversation. Apologize if you realize you offended them, said something unwise, or hurt them. Sometimes you may have said the right thing in the correct way, but they were still hurt. You shouldn't apologize for saying what needed to be said if it was done in a loving and gracious way. But please consider acknowledging how difficult this must be for them or that you're sorry for what they're going through.

Carefully Consider Any Decisions
After the Conversation

If you must make a decision after the conversation, move slowly. In regard to decisions, pastor and leadership expert Dr. John Maxwell said that they "should always be made as close to the problem as possible."[11] The closer you are to the problem, the closer you are to the person you're engaging and to reaching your goal.

When we have difficult conversations, Darrell Bock identified four filters that form our ethical choices: "(1) the content; (2) the weighing of the content; (3) the person/people being engaged; (4) and the impact on the community."[12] Darrell was spot-on with his filters, but I want to take what he suggested, rewrite them as questions, and add a few more questions:

- What's involved in the decision I'm about to make?
- How could this decision be interpreted by different people?
- Who's being engaged, and what's their story?
- How will this affect the community and/or my relationships?
- What does Scripture say about the topic?
- Where is the tension of this decision?
- How might this decision point more people to Jesus?

Regardless of your decision, there is the possibility that the person might walk away. And if that is indeed the case, the best thing to do is let them make the decisions they're going to make. If I've learned anything over the past few years, it's this: *when people walk away, let them go!* Not everyone who comes into your life is "family." (If you count most people who walk into your life as family, you appreciate your actual family and good friends less.) Some friends who walk into your life are forever. Some are a gift for a season. Chaos arises when you try to make seasonal friends fit the mold of lifelong ones. Whenever I've attempted to stop someone from leaving a friendship or from church, the result has been more disastrous than had I just let them go. Also, letting people go freely makes it easier for them to freely return (if they so desire). Dr. Henry Cloud and Dr. John Townsend gave us these words of encouragement:

> A successful confrontation will always involve balancing grace and truth. Grace is your being on the side of, or "for," the other person as well as the relationship. Truth is the reality of whatever you need to say about the problem. This balancing combination is referred to as being *neutralized*.
>
> Being *neutralized* doesn't mean being *neutral* about the problem—not taking a side or expressing an opinion. In fact, the clearer you express your opinion, the better your chances of success. Instead, being neutralized means that having grace and truth together counters the bad effects of having one of these by itself. In other words, grace alone or truth alone can have a negative effect in a confrontation.[13]

Hopefully, this conversation is one of many to come. I trust that as you have each conversation, the outcome will look better and better.

12

ARE YOU A GUIDE OR A GATEKEEPER?

The road was dark. It seemed like the outside darkness was literally swallowing the car's headlights. If that wasn't enough reason to panic, my cell phone wasn't showing any signal, and there was little sign of life in the houses alongside of the road. Nonetheless, I pressed on toward my destination. Far from being lost, I knew my location. I drove these roads at least once a week during my sophomore and junior years of college.

My headlights started to reveal a white gravel road up ahead that seemingly emerged out of nowhere. The combination of the car lights and white gravel gave the road a ghostly appearance. Nothing distinguished the gravel road from similar roads I had just passed, but I knew this was the road I should turn left on.

Slowing down to almost a stop, I turned left and cautiously began traveling down the road. The tires picked up the gravel and chucked it underneath and behind my car. After about fifteen seconds, I began to see an old country church in the distance.

I parked with my headlights shining on the building. There it was: the place where I preached for eighteen months so long ago. I still remember being a sophomore in college and feeling excited that church leaders invited me to be their pastor. Because the church was only seventy-five miles north of my college, it wouldn't be too difficult to be involved in the lives of the people, a community with much potential. To this day, I have photos of the members, my sermon outlines, and some fond memories. I learned how to do hospital visits, comfort people, and pray for those who were mourning. I started to understand how to connect with members during the week, and most importantly, I cut my teeth on preaching. I mastered some valuable lessons while pastoring that church.

There were also several unexpected lessons afforded to me during my tenure at the church. I painfully discovered that church leadership wasn't the primrose path I had once assumed. A younger and more naive me speculated that the life of a pastor would have challenging seasons, but I was clueless about the dire experiences that would occur again and again. The church's elders were among the first to show me what a gut-wrenching ministry experience felt like.

I remember the day. After eighteen months of inviting my mother to attend my church and hear me preach, she finally gave in. The following Sunday, she didn't return, but the church elders met with me and told me not to bring people like her if I wanted to keep my job. Needless to say, I immediately submitted my resignation. I wrote about this experience with more detail in *Messy Grace.* Lamenting what could have been at this church, I wrote, "To this day, I have not returned to see what happened to that church. Maybe one day I will. I hope they are different."[1]

More than twenty-two years later, the church was different, but *not* better.

The longer I stared at the building, the more my heart dropped to my stomach. Even though the church had recently closed, the actual building started falling apart years ago. Paint was peeling off, roof shingles hung by a thread, the porch had holes, and doors were padlocked shut. A tear emerged in the corner of my eye as I started to think about the church's history. In the early 1900s, someone or a group of Christians decided to start a church in this small Missouri town (the population was probably higher than it is now). They were likely eager and excited as they dreamed about what the church would do for Jesus. I'm sure they had no idea that a hundred years or so later, the church would just fade away—quietly.

Except for the light from my car, the town was dark. The air outside was cold and silent. To be honest, the silence was unsettling, almost as if mourning what the church once was. The deteriorating building served as a metaphor of what could have been.

BACK IN THE CHURCH CONFERENCE ROOM

At the start of the first chapter, I left you with a cliff-hanger. I was meeting with a group of church leaders who were baffled when two married lesbian couples with young children came to the conviction that marriage was between a man and woman and wanted the leadership to advise them of what to do next. I posed this question: "What would you do?"

And so now I'll explain what I did. Near the end of my meeting with these church leaders, I helped them determine some suggestions for possible ways forward:

- Take more time to pray.
- Go over what the Bible says about relationships and sexuality.
- Don't make a decision until you have certainty that faith provides.
- Examine the financial and insurance needs of each individual.

I warned the church leaders against just advising the couples to divorce and trust God. While we should always trust God, there were young children from a foster system involved, and they, above all others, deserved the gift of intentionality.

> Too many people believe that self-focus and personal satisfaction bring everything together in the end, but it's a lie.

Eventually, both couples ended up divorcing. They decided this on their own and were not manipulated into doing so. Even though the couples divorced, they remained living together as friends and roommates to keep consistency for their children. When it came to sexual temptation, the women said they hadn't been sexually intimate for a few years. Today both couples and their children are still part of the church. When people who relate or identify as LGBTQ request spiritual guidance or have questions about faith and sexuality, the church sends them to the four women for counsel.

Was their outcome perfect? *Nope.*

Is the situation messy? *Sure is. And so are you.*

Are their lives easier? *No. Jesus promised peace, not ease.*

Is God using them? *More than you know.*

When I tell this story, it shocks most people. I think it's because of the kind of society we're living in: one with a modern view and scientism mindset that urges people to focus on the tyranny of self. "Far from delivering pleasure and happiness, this strategy of living for self has brought about discontent and depression."[2] Too many people believe that self-focus and personal satisfaction bring everything together in the end, but it's a lie. A relentless focus on others and commitment to community makes it easier for people to find and follow Jesus.

Thankfully, as a teenager, I discovered a community that I fell in love with, even before I was a Christian. Though my Christian brothers and sisters have hurt me and I've hurt them, my love for the church is stronger than ever. As the son of three LGBTQ parents, when I first went to church, I wasn't sure what to expect or what I'd find. The more I attended church, the more fascinating people I met. Throughout the years, I've met many gatekeepers, but I wish I'd stumbled across more guides.

GATEKEEPERS

Not long ago, I flew out of state to speak at a conference. I didn't sleep well the night I arrived, and I awoke earlier than usual the first morning of the conference. I decided to arrive early to the conference, well before my call time. I noticed that a friend of mine was in the speakers' lounge and would be presenting as well. Later, at his session, he shared his testimony of growing up in the church, never trusting Jesus during childhood, going to college, being in a same-sex relationship, and finally trusting Jesus. At the end of the session, my friend talked about his conviction not to be in same-sex relationships and to be celibate. To say his story was moving would be an understatement. Because his session had already been posted to social media, I decided to share it on my social-media accounts.

Within an hour of posting, I received a private message from someone venting about how wrong I was for posting my friend's message. The individual who wrote the private message also mentioned that my friend's words endangered LGBTQ children and students. I started to get frustrated as I thought more about the private message. When my friend shared his story, at no time were others belittled or shamed, but I was still haunted by the possibility that my friend's story was abusive. Later that night, there was still a small voice inside me saying, "You've endangered the next generation." After reflecting and praying, I came back to my senses. My friend's story wasn't wrong or hurtful; quite the contrary, his testimony actually gave many people hope because it highlighted God's unconditional love. It's amazing how one private message triggered my insecurities and activated my "people pleasing" mode, huh? Actually, it was more than just a private message; it was a gatekeeper pressuring me with his assumptions and misguided view of love.

> If someone uses scare tactics (guilt, fear, name calling, and so forth) to pressure you into changing your views, they are probably a gatekeeper.

The idea that people can't love each other while disagreeing about what the Bible teaches about relationships and sexuality is not only extreme but nonsensical. The mindset that anyone who has a narrow view of marriage is unintelligent, out of touch, bigoted, or abusive is ridiculous at best and grotesque at worst. Gatekeepers make such flawed and untrue arguments popular today. They rely on logical fallacies like straw-man arguments, faulty analogies, hasty generalizations, personal incredulity, and undistributed middle terms. They attempt to persuade others with an either-or choice—a false dichotomy. False dichotomies give rise to the inaccurate belief that people won't have a voice unless they take an extremist position for one side or the other. Gatekeepers are why so many false dichotomies exist in our society.

If someone uses scare tactics (guilt, fear, name calling, and so forth) to pressure you into changing your views, they are probably a gatekeeper. They operate from an us-versus-them mentality (making assumptions about and mistreating others in the exact way they fear being mistreated). Posing as valiant sufferers (martyrs), they champion whatever issue they're passionate about. In order to be seen as heroes and dogmatically correct, villains must be manufactured. Anyone holding an opposing view is automatically demonized, as is the view. Clash with a gatekeeper over their hobbyhorse and they'll brand your view as harmful! Unless you're on your game, without even knowing it, you've already been steered into a relational false dichotomy in which you feel as though you have two options:

1. Walk away from the gatekeeper and don't look back. While this option may look attractive (and there are some toxic people that you should distance yourself from), most of the time, we're just running from difficult people. In Matthew 5:38–48 and Luke 6:35–36, Jesus implores us to do the exact opposite: love, serve, and walk next to them. Keep difficult people in your life because they give you a chance to be more like Jesus.

2. Maintain a relationship with the gatekeeper by adopting the gatekeeper's view. The catch is that your relationship with the gatekeeper will be either short lived or extremely shallow. You're merely another trophy on the shelf of their insecurity. You've also emboldened their false-dichotomy view and enabled them to search for the next scalp. Worse yet, you've compromised your character by shifting your view to keep the relationship. Never shift theological convictions to resolve tension in your relationships. Eventually, you'll regret your decision and may even come to resent those around you.

There's a third option: risk losing your relationship with the gatekeeper by holding firm to your view (maintaining your character) and keep them in your life. Will gatekeepers label you? Probably. They may lie about you, but you will have refrained from participating in their false dichotomy. People will notice you haven't taken sides and might be prompted not to do so either. You'll also have the opportunity to continue loving the gatekeeper regardless of how you were treated.

Obviously, there are Christian gatekeepers too. Not all conservative Christians picket parades or bully on social media. But are there examples of parents who mishandled their child's coming out? *Without question.* Have people been treated poorly for their views about marriage or the LGBTQ reality? *Absolutely.* Can we name circumstances in which people have been indifferent toward LGBTQ individuals and caused them pain? *All too often.*

Those examples are not reflective of every scenario (and I would go so far as to say they aren't even a majority of scenarios).

While multiple heartrending stories and ugly statistics keep us praying, gatekeepers rarely mention the countless stories of parents and children who have harmonious relationships despite differing views on sexual intimacy and marriage. Friends who have opposing theological convictions on whether gender is malleable remain as close as ever. Trans men and women still have substantial and loving relationships with family members who urged them not to undergo sex-reassignment surgery.

Encouraging stories aren't reported enough, and those that are go vastly uncelebrated. Gatekeepers appear to be more numerous than they actually are because their voices are loud. And loud voices are hardly ever empathetic. Society's climate would vastly improve if we adjusted our perspective from *either-or* to *everyone*. Christians need to think more deeply about people, not differently about theology. Instead of being a gatekeeper, you need to be willing to compassionately navigate people through society.

GUIDES

The ever-increasing gap between some LGBTQ individuals and some churches continues to damage more people and families than we will probably ever realize. Pastor and speaker Carey Nieuwhof wrote, "Broken people have come to the end of themselves and learned there was not much there in the first place. Broken people get to the point that they realize the poverty within and have to look beyond themselves for renewal and strength."[3] Whereas everyone needs to focus on Jesus as their ultimate source of renewal and strength, we must also look to Jesus through the example of another person: *a guide.* Even Paul told the Corinthian believers, "Follow my example, as I follow the example of Christ" (1 Corinthians 11:1).

Donald Miller, when helping organizations build their brand, helps people understand the importance of *guides* as opposed to *heroes.* Miller contends that heroes are not always the strongest characters. Rather, the guide "has already 'been there and done that' and has conquered the hero's challenge in their own backstory. The guide, not the hero, is the one with the most authority. Still, the story is rarely about the guide. The guide simply plays a role."[4] Think about the guides in movies and books: Shuri and Nick Fury (*Marvel Cinematic Universe* series), Mr. Keating (*Dead Poets Society*), Mr. Miyagi (*The Karate Kid* movies and *Cobra Kai* series), Mary Poppins, Gandalf (*The Hobbit* and *The Lord of the Rings* series), Professor McGonagall and Dumbledore (the *Harry Potter* series), Yoda and Obi-Wan Kenobi (the *Star Wars* saga), Mickey Goldmill and Apollo Creed (*Rocky* series), Morpheus (*The Matrix* series) . . . And as you can tell, the list can go on!

> Whereas everyone needs to look to Jesus as their source of renewal and strength, broken individuals need to start by looking at another person: a guide.

Specifically, guides are the complete opposite of gatekeepers. Guides do the following:

- inspire people to follow them
- lead by example instead of dictating direction
- know and understand the boundaries
- value the truth about boundaries

- warn about going beyond the boundaries
- set the example
- don't outpace those following them
- pay attention to how their followers are doing
- walk with others
- share helpful advice
- understand that people take different journeys to the destination

Again, this particular idea of guides that I'm proposing isn't new. Attempting to guide believers in Corinth, Paul pleaded with them to imitate him as he imitated Jesus (see 1 Corinthians 11:1). He wasn't afraid to openly discuss his previous failures or current struggles. Instead of giving into an egotistical need to be seen as one with authority, Paul presented himself as a weak individual who fully relied on Jesus (see 2 Corinthians 12:9–13). Guides understand what my friend Dusty Frizzell once preached in a sermon: "Being human takes humility."[5] Humility is what distinguishes guides from gatekeepers. It's why guides have considerably more influence than gatekeepers.

Gatekeepers detest being seen as mere humans. Resist the urge to stabilize your insecurities by imitating gatekeepers. This only produces a false resolution to the felt tension of loving God and people at the same time. Losing influence isn't worth becoming like the gatekeepers. Imitating the very people who fought against Jesus isn't worth it.

REMEMBER, ALL FOR THE SAKE OF INFLUENCE

Throughout the years, more than a few Christians have failed LGBTQ individuals (an understatement). Author and speaker Christopher Yuan indicated that some Christians have inappropriately sought to resolve their frustration with same-sex attraction by using reparative therapy in order to shift a person's sexual orientation. As you likely know, therapy aimed at changing orientation does a tremendous amount of harm to an individual. The goal isn't orientation change but rather *life change*—life change as in growing closer to Jesus. Yuan wrote, "Sanctification is not getting rid of our temptations, but pursuing holiness in the midst of them. If our goal is making people straight, then we are practicing a false gospel."[6] The endgame has never been to make gay people straight but rather to help everyone primarily identify with Jesus. Since Genesis 3, humanity has competed against Jesus for the spotlight of their main identity. Whether sexuality, career, ideas, politics, family, relationships, or _____ (you fill in the blank), people have attempted to maneuver anything to take center stage.

God himself is the only One strong enough to shoulder the responsibility for our primary identification. One way or another, our identity will crush anything that tries to bear its weight. Because Jesus died and rose for us, he alone gets to define us. He's the One who has qualified us in the relationship, so we don't get the privilege of qualifying our relationship with him.

Those of us who follow Jesus have a responsibility to help guide others to him regardless of our life circumstances, but we cannot accomplish Jesus's mission alone. We need the church. Author and pastor Ed Stetzer pointed out that "you simply can't be a good neighbor who engages the world without the support of the local church."[7] As such, the church needs to be a place where people can belong before they belong, because as I stated earlier, people find and follow Jesus better with community than in isolation. The church needs to make it as easy as possible for people to find Jesus, because it sure can be difficult to follow him at times.

That is why it's imperative for the church to be a gathering that offers belonging. It's belonging that inspires people to grow. My friends Becket Cook, Brian Buxton, Rachel, Michael, and others would agree.

Think about how much influence the men and women in Becket's church had in his life. How Becket described his church should be the description for all churches: a place where anyone can attend and encounter love, truth, grace, authenticity, integrity, empathy, and compassion. We have a glimpse of what the church should look like through the image of God in each of us.

> Those of us who follow Jesus have a responsibility to help guide others to him regardless of our life circumstances.

Former president of Fuller Theological Seminary, Richard Mouw inferred that the image of God "has a 'corporate' dimension. . . . By looking at different individuals and groups we get glimpses of different aspects of the full image of God."[8] I like Mouw's thinking; it's almost as if he was having us imagine a stained-glass mosaic of different colors, shapes, sizes, and designs.

When Christians come together, each possessing their unique spiritual gifts and personality, something special happens. It's almost as if all the diverse Lego pieces join and everything is awesome! Mouw's words also remind me of one of the most beautiful illustrations in Scripture:

> There before me was a great multitude that no one could count, from every nation, tribe, people and language, standing before the throne and before the Lamb. They were wearing white robes and were holding palm branches in their hands. And they cried out in a loud voice:
>
> > "Salvation belongs to our God,
> > who sits on the throne,
> > and to the Lamb." (Revelation 7:9–10)

Such a diverse picture of people is so powerful that it has been known to influence even the hardest of hearts. The belonging that we read about throughout the Bible is what God wants to offer LGBTQ individuals. Bible scholar Eugene Peterson paraphrased Paul's God-inspired words in Romans 9:25–26: "I'll call nobodies and make them somebodies; I'll call the unloved and make them beloved. In the place where they yelled out, 'You're nobody!' they're calling you 'God's living children'" (MSG).

WHAT ARE *YOU* WILLING TO DO?

In fall 2015, around the same time as the release of *Messy Grace*, I started a unique small group. I gathered a group of a dozen individuals (mostly millennials and Gen Zers) who attended the church I was leading and related in some way as LGBTQ. The plan was for us to meet for two hours every Tuesday night for about four months. I promised that I wouldn't try to "de-gay" them but that I just wanted to hear their stories and talk about Jesus.

After a month, our group grew to about fifteen people. Some were in same-sex relationships, some were in between relationships, some were celibate because of their theological convictions, and some were confused about their identity. Christians had wounded each person in the group at some point or another (maybe when they came out to people or shared their attraction with someone). During the final meeting, I asked them, "Why do you attend our church if you know we have differences regarding marriage?"

Their answers were so intriguing. Here's what they said:

- "Most 'gay churches' talk a lot about being gay. I'm gay, so I don't need to talk about it."
- "Many 'gay churches' don't preach the gospel."
- "We don't have to believe everything a church believes to attend; we just have to know we're welcome."
- "I've felt as though God hated me. Do you know what it's like to sing worship songs to someone you feel hates you? Now, for the first time in a long time, I believe God loves me."

Two young women who were dating stayed behind after everyone left that final meeting. Though they loved each other, they said that after studying so much about Jesus, they had doubts about whether or not they should continue dating.

"Can we talk to you about it?" one of them asked with tears in her eyes.

Truth felt messy in that moment as my eyes welled up. We began what

> Compassion for anyone definitely seems messy, because people are messy.

turned out to be a four-hour conversation. If I had just told the group members what to believe or rushed them, my conversation with these women probably never would've happened. I had many of the other conversations held within the bond of that group. I chose to fight for influence—to be a guide instead of a gatekeeper. I hope you'll do the same.

Convictions about God's words can feel messy.

Compassion for anyone definitely seems messy, because people are messy.

Conversations with everyone are messy. They hardly go as planned.

Truth may feel and look messy, but it isn't. God's truth is pure, trustworthy, altogether right, and is best discerned and lived out with others. The more we value community and bringing others in, the easier it will be for people to find and follow Jesus.

Before I end, I'll pose this question once more: "What are you willing to do to keep and build influence with _____?"

ACKNOWLEDGMENTS

Thank you to the following people:

- Amy, Joel, Rachel, and Oscar K the Basenji—you are my squad, and I love you more than you know. I'm thankful for your patience with me during the long days and, often, long nights of writing and developing content.
- Don Gates—you are more than an agent, more than a leader, more than a strategist; you've become a really good friend.
- Susan Tjaden, Laura Wright, Paul Pastor, Brett Benson, Douglas Mann, Julie Smyth, Cara Iverson, and others at WaterBrook Multnomah—I appreciate all the hard work you've done to make this project a reality. You are level 5 leaders. And to Susan specifically: once my people, always my people.
- Becket Cook, Ruth Malhotra, Tyler Chernesky, Chris Marlin, Brian Buxton—our conversations have helped me develop the principles in this book. I'm grateful.

- Ray Johnston—for being a mentor and friend in this new season.

- The churches and organizations I've consulted with and spoken for—countless hours of conversations and strategy sessions with hundreds of churches of various sizes, schools, and ministries is helping me know how to guide others to love God and people well.

NOTES

Chapter 1: How Far Are You Willing to Go?

1. See Plato, *Gorgias* 453b–465e.
2. Tyler Coates, "J. K. Rowling Wants You to Know How Gay Dumbledore Really Was," *Esquire,* March 18, 2019, www.esquire.com/entertainment/books/a26858267/j-k-rowling-dumbledore-grindelwald-gay-harry-potter.
3. Lisa Respers France, "J. K. Rowling Responds to Gay Dumbledore Controversy," CNN, February 2, 2018, www.cnn.com/2018/02/01/entertainment/jk-rowling-dumbledore-gay/index.html.

Chapter 2: What Is Messy Truth?

1. Becket Cook, quoted in Sophia Lee, "Freedom for the Same-Sex Attracted," *World,* September 25, 2015, https://world.wng.org/2015/09/freedom_for_the_same_sex_attracted.
2. Becket Cook and Brett McCracken, "From Gay to Gospel: The Fascinating Story of Becket Cook," *Gospel Coalition,* August 23, 2019, www.thegospelcoalition.org/article/gay-gospel-becket-cook.
3. Becket Cook, quoted in Jonathan Parks-Ramage, "Jesus, Mary, and Joe Jonas: A Journey into Reality L.A., Hollywood's Hippest Evangelical Church," *Medium,* March 7, 2018, https://medium.com/s/losing-my-religion/jesus-mary-and-joe-jonas-605c763ce682.

4. Becket Cook, *A Change of Affection: A Gay Man's Incredible Story of Redemption* (Nashville: Thomas Nelson, 2019), 16.

5. Dr. Joel Hoomans, "35,000 Decisions: The Great Choices of Strategic Leaders," *Leading Edge,* March 20, 2015, https://go.roberts.edu/leadingedge/the-great-choices-of-strategic-leaders.

6. Charles Duhigg, *The Power of Habit: Why We Do What We Do in Life and Business* (New York: Random House, 2014), 17–18.

7. Horst Balz and Gerhard Schneider, eds., *Exegetical Dictionary of the New Testament* (Grand Rapids, MI: Eerdmans, 1993), 3:137.

8. Robert A. J. Gagnon, *The Bible and Homosexual Practice: Texts and Hermeneutics* (Nashville: Abingdon, 2001), 191.

9. Frank Turek, "LGBTQ Contradictions," *Cross Examined* (blog), August 4, 2016, https://crossexamined.org/lgbtq-contradictions.

10. Eve Tushnet, "I'm Gay, but I'm Not Switching to a Church That Supports Gay Marriage," *Atlantic,* May 30, 2013, www.theatlantic.com/sexes/archive/2013/05/im-gay-but-im-not-switching-to-a-church-that-supports-gay-marriage/276383.

Chapter 3: What's the Value of Anyone?

1. Francis Brown, Samuel Driver, and Charles Briggs, eds., *Enhanced Brown-Driver-Briggs Hebrew and English Lexicon* (Oxford: Clarendon Press, 1977), 854; James Swanson, "1952 תּוּמָד," *Dictionary of Biblical Languages with Semantic Domains: Hebrew (Old Testament)* (Oak Harbor, WA: Logos Research Systems, 1997), with the exact definition being "that which has a similarity or comparison, image, form, what is seen, builder's draft, sketch, a graphic representation for building a construction, figurine"; and Swanson, "7512 I. סֶלֶף."

2. Peggy Shinn, "How Bruce Jenner Became 'the World's Greatest Athlete,'" Team USA, April 30, 2015, www.teamusa.org/News/2015/April/30/How-Bruce-Jenner-Became-The-Worlds-Greatest-Athlete.

3. Buzz Bissinger, "Caitlyn Jenner: The Full Story," *Vanity Fair,* June 25, 2015, www.vanityfair.com/hollywood/2015/06/caitlyn-jenner-bruce-cover-annie-leibovitz.

4. Bruce Jenner and Diane Sawyer, quoted in Daniella Diaz, "Bruce Jenner Comes Out . . . as a Republican," interview by Diane Saw-

yer, CNN, April 25, 2015, www.cnn.com/2015/04/25/politics/
bruce-jenner-diane-sawyer-transgender-lgbt-republican
-conservative/index.html.

5. Caitlyn Jenner, quoted in Carly Mallenbaum, "Caitlyn Jenner: It
Was Easy to Come Out Trans; Hard to Come Out Republican,"
USA Today, July 20, 2016, www.usatoday.com/story/news/politics/
onpolitics/2016/07/20/caitlyn-jenner-rnc-trump-cleveland/8733
7344.

6. Rose McGowan, quoted in Katia Hetter, "Rose McGowan: Caitlyn Jenner Doesn't Understand 'Being a Woman,'" *CNN,* No-
vember 18, 2015, www.cnn.com/2015/11/18/entertainment/caitlin
-jenner-rose-mcgowan-criticism-feat.

7. Caitlyn Jenner, "Caitlyn Jenner Discusses Marriage on The Ellen
Show!" YouTube video, 3:38, posted by "Caitlyn Jenner," September 6, 2015, www.youtube.com/watch?v=5Eyqt8X_WiU.

8. Ellen DeGeneres, quoted in Megan French, "Caitlyn Jenner Slams
Ellen DeGeneres in New Memoir: Report," *Us Weekly,* April 13,
2017, www.usmagazine.com/celebrity-news/news/caitlyn-jenner
-slams-ellen-degeneres-in-new-memoir-report-w476642.

9. Christopher Dean Hopkins, "Jenner: 'For All Intents and Purposes,
I Am a Woman,'" *NPR,* April 24, 2015, www.npr.org/sections/
thetwo-way/2015/04/24/402069597/jenner-for-all-intents-and
-purposes-i-am-a-woman.

10. Angus Stevenson, ed., *Oxford Dictionary of English,* 3rd ed. (New
York: Oxford University Press, 2010), 869, s.v. "identity," www
.lexico.com/definition/identity.

11. *Merriam-Webster,* s.v. "identity," www.merriam-webster.com/
dictionary/identity.

12. Mark A. Yarhouse and Lori A. Burkett, *Sexual Identity: A Guide to
Living in the Time Between the Times* (Lanham, MD: University
Press of America, 2003), 6.

13. When the created want to be the Creator, they must place themselves at the center of their lives. I believe this is one of the reasons
Paul mentioned in Romans 1:25 that the created worship the created (themselves, other creatures, and noncreatures).

14. Greg Johnson, "I Used to Hide My Shame. Now I Take Shelter
Under the Gospel," *Christianity Today,* May 20, 2019, www

.christianitytoday.com/ct/2019/may-web-only/greg-johnson
-hide-shame-shelter-gospel-gay-teenager.html.

15. See Ann P. Haas, Jody L. Herman, and Philip L. Rodgers, *Suicide Attempts Among Transgender and Gender Non-Conforming Adults: Findings of the National Transgender Discrimination Survey*, Williams Institute and American Foundation for Suicide Prevention (January 2014), 12, www.familleslgbt.org/1463149763/Haas%20 2014.pdf; Jody L. Herman, Taylor N. T. Brown, and Ann P. Haas, "Suicide Thoughts and Attempts Among Transgender Adults: Findings from the 2015 U.S. Transgender Survey," UCLA and Williams Institute (September 2019), https://williamsinstitute.law .ucla.edu/wp-content/uploads/AFSP-Williams-Suicide-Report-Final .pdf; and Sandy E. James et al., *The Report of the 2015 U.S. Transgender Survey* (Washington, DC: National Center for Transgender Equality, 2016), https://transequality.org/sites/default/files/docs/ usts/USTS-Full-Report-Dec17.pdf.

Chapter 4: Will You Trust What Jesus Says Even When You Disagree with Him?

1. In the first century, the people didn't have Scripture divided into verses and chapters as we do today.

2. René Gehring, *The Biblical "One Flesh" Theology of Marriage as Constituted in Genesis 2:24: An Exegetical Study of This Human-Divine Covenant Pattern, Its New Testament Echoes, and Its Reception History Throughout Scripture* (PhD thesis, Avondale College, 2011), 320, https://research.avondale.edu.au/theses_phd/1.

3. For further discussion , see Kenneth A. Mathews, *The New American Commentary: An Exegetical and Theological Exposition of Holy Scripture: Genesis 1–11:26, Vol. 1A,* New International Version (Nashville: Broadman, Holman, 1996), 222. See also R. Laird Harris, Gleason L. Archer Jr., and Bruce K. Waltke, eds., *Theological Wordbook of the Old Testament* (Chicago: Moody, 1999), 658–59, on the NIV word *unite:* "This word is also used figuratively with man as the subject. He can forsake, i.e. apostatize. Israel is indicted for this on numerous occasions (Deut 28:20; 31:16; Jud 10:10; Jer 1:16). In forsaking the Lord and following

after idols she was guilty of breaking the covenant (Jon 2:8; Deut 29:24; I Kgs 19:10, 14) and of adultery (Hos 4:10)."

4. Jesus's answers to the Pharisees remind the reader of Malachi 2. Pleading with Israel to stay faithful to God, Malachi appealed to God's creation of humanity and the marriage covenant: "Do we not all have one Father? Did not one God create us? . . . Has not the one God made you? You belong to him in body and spirit. And what does the one God seek? Godly offspring. So be on your guard, and do not be unfaithful to the wife of your youth" (verses 10, 15).

5. In the next chapter of 1 Corinthians, Paul warned married believers about abstaining from sex with their spouse for too long and advised single believers to get married if they were burning with lust (7:5, 9).

6. F. F. Bruce, *The Epistles to the Colossians, to Philemon, and to the Ephesians,* The New International Commentary on the New Testament (Grand Rapids, MI: Eerdmans, 1984), 394–95. Bruce suggested that Genesis 2:24 is best understood as fulfilled in Christ's marriage to his bride, the church. Bruce said that this mystery "could not be understood until Christ, who loved his people from eternity, gave himself up for them in the fullness of time. . . . His people constitute his bride, united to him in 'one body.' The formation of Eve to be Adam's companion is seen to prefigure the creation of the church to be the bride of Christ."

7. William J. Webb, *Slaves, Women, and Homosexuals: Exploring the Hermeneutics of Cultural Analysis* (Downer's Grove, IL: Inter-Varsity, 2001), 24, 31, 52.

8. Darrell Bock, "Sexuality and the Church—Stanton Jones and Mark Yarhouse," YouTube video, 48:54, posted by "Dallas Theological Seminary," September 17, 2014, www.youtube.com/watch?v=AE_AsRu00Ok.

9. Preston Sprinkle, *People to Be Loved: Why Homosexuality Is Not Just an Issue* (Grand Rapids, MI: Zondervan, 2015), 70.

10. John L. Allen Jr., "Interview with Anglican Bishop N. T. Wright of Durham, England," *National Catholic Reporter,* May 21, 2004, http://www.nationalcatholicreporter.org/word/wright.htm.

11. There are several examples of monogamous same-sex relationships

in Jesus's day. Many appear in ancient Greek writings. Some well-known couples are Harmodius and Aristogeiton, Pelopidas and Epaminondas, and Alexander and Bagoas. It should be noted that in these examples, the Greek word for "marriage" is hardly ever mentioned or does not appear at all. The Romans seem to be some of the first to perform some sort of same-sex marriages. Some mentions in current scholarship include Thomas K. Hubbard, ed., *Homosexuality in Greece and Rome: A Sourcebook of Basic Documents* (Berkeley: University of California Press, 2003), 5–6; Bernadette J. Brooten, *Love Between Women: Early Christian Responses to Female Homoeroticism,* The Chicago Series on Sexuality, History, and Society (University of Chicago Press, 1996), 3; Robert A. J. Gagnon, *The Bible and Homosexual Practice: Texts and Hermeneutics* (Nashville: Abingdon, 2001), 350–60; Robert A. J. Gagnon, "A Book Not to Be Embraced: A Critical Appraisal on Stacy Johnson's *A Time to Embrace*," *Scottish Journal of Theology* 26, no. 1 (February 2009), 61–80 (or see http://robgagnon .net/articles/homosexStacyJohnsonSJT2.pdf); William Loader, *The New Testament on Sexuality: Attitudes Towards Sexuality in Judaism and Christianity in the Hellenistic Greco-Roman Era* (Grand Rapids, MI: Eerdmans, 2012), 84, 324–25; Mark D. Smith, "Ancient Bisexuality and the Interpretation of Romans 1.26, 27," *Journal of the American Academy of Religion* (1996), 64:235–37; and Bruce S. Thornton, *Eros: The Myth of Ancient Greek Sexuality* (New York: Routledge, 1998), 105–8.

12.   For a good understanding of marriage and sexuality in the first-century Roman Empire, see Joseph D. Fantin, "Sexualities in the First-Century World: A Survey of Relevant Topics," in *Sanctified Sexuality: Valuing Sex in an Oversexed World,* ed. Sandra L. Glahn & C. Gary Barnes (Grand Rapids, MI: Kregel, 2020), 55–60.

13.   Barry Corey, *Love Kindness: Discover the Power of a Forgotten Christian Virtue* (Carol Stream, IL: Tyndale, 2019), 60.

Chapter 5: When Does Belonging Happen?

1.   *Cambridge Dictionary,* s.v. "belong," https://dictionary.cambridge .org/us/dictionary/english/belong?q=Belonging.

2.   *Oxford Dictionary,* s.v. "belonging," https://en.oxforddictionaries .com/definition/belonging.

3. Stanley Hauerwas, quoted in Peter Mommsen, "Why Community Is Dangerous: An Interview with Stanley Hauerwas," *Plough Quarterly,* May 19, 2016, www.plough.com/en/topics/community/church-community/why-community-is-dangerous.

4. Dr. Heather Looy, quoted in Mark A. Yarhouse, *Understanding Gender Dysphoria: Navigating Transgender Issues in a Changing Culture,* Christian Association for Psychological Studies Books (Downer's Grove, IL: InterVarsity, 2015), 38.

5. Lucy Knight, "Being a Gay Christian Can Be Hurtful and Gruelling. But I Refuse to Lose Faith," *Guardian,* March 21, 2019, www.theguardian.com/commentisfree/2019/mar/21/gay-christian-church-lgbt.

6. Frederick William Danker, ed., *A Greek-English Lexicon of the New Testament and Other Early Christian Literature,* 3rd ed. (University of Chicago Press, 2000), 468.

7. Horst Balz and Gerhard Schneider, eds., *Exegetical Dictionary of the New Testament* (Grand Rapids, MI: Eerdmans, 1990), 1:121.

8. Gordon D. Fee, *The First Epistle to the Corinthians* (Grand Rapids, MI: Eerdmans, 1987), 672.

Chapter 6: Acknowledging Other People's Experience

1. Brené Brown, *Daring Greatly: How the Courage to Be Vulnerable Transforms the Way We Live, Love, Parent, and Lead* (New York: Avery, 2015), 81.

2. Brené Brown, *Dare to Lead: Brave Work. Tough Conversations. Whole Hearts* (New York: Random House, 2018), 202. Brown went on to say, "If I'm sharing something that's difficult, I need to make space for people to feel the way they feel—in contrast to either punishing them for having those feelings because I'm uncomfortable, or trying to caretake and rescue them from their feelings," 202.

3. See Sandy E. James et al., *The Report of the 2015 U.S. Transgender Survey* (Washington, DC: National Center for Transgender Equality, 2016), 115, 132–37, https://transequality.org/sites/default/files/docs/usts/USTS-Full-Report-Dec17.pdf; and Ann P. Haas, Jody L. Herman, and Philip L. Rodgers, "Suicide Attempts Among Transgender and Gender Non-Conforming Adults: Find-

ings of the National Transgender Discrimination Survey," The Williams Institute and American Foundation for Suicide Prevention, 5–8, https://williamsinstitute.law.ucla.edu/wp-content/uploads/AFSP-Williams-Suicide-Report-Final.pdf.

4. See Walt Heyer, "Hormones, Surgery, Regret: I Was a Transgender Woman for 8 Years—Time I Can't Get Back," *USA Today*, February 11, 2019, www.usatoday.com/story/opinion/voices/2019/02/11/transgender-debate-transitioning-sex-gender-column/1894076002; Friedemann Pfäfflin, "Regrets After Sex Reassignment Surgery," *Journal of Psychology and Human Sexuality* 5, no. 4 (May 1993), 69–85; and Emer Scully, "Hundreds of Transgender Youths Who Had Gender Reassignment Surgery Wish They Hadn't and Want to Transition Back, Says Trans Rights Champion," *Daily Mail*, October 7, 2019, www.dailymail.co.uk/news/article-7541679/Hundreds-youths-gender-surgery-wish-hadnt-says-head-advocacy-network.html.

5. See Cecilia Dhejne et al., "Long-Term Follow-Up of Transsexual Persons Undergoing Sex Reassignment Surgery: Cohort Study in Sweden," *PLOS One* 6, no. 2 (2011), https://doi.org/10.1371/journal.pone.0016885; Haas, Herman, and Rodgers, "Suicide Attempts," 8–9; Noah Adams, Maaya Hitomi, and Cherie Moody, "Varied Reports of Adult Transgender Suicidality: Synthesizing and Describing the Peer-Reviewed and Gray Literature," *Transgender Health* 2, no. 1 (April 1, 2017), 60–75; and Michal Avrech Bar et al., "Male-to-female Transitions: Implications for Occupational Performance, Health, and Life Satisfaction," *The Canadian Journal of Occupational Therapy* 83, no. 2 (2016), 72–82, https://doi.org/10.1177/0008417416635346.

6. Malcolm Gladwell, *Outliers: The Story of Success* (New York: Little, Brown, 2008), 221.

7. Linda Greenhouse, "Black Robes Don't Make the Justice, but the Rest of the Closet Just Might," *New York Times*, December 4, 2002, www.nytimes.com/2002/12/04/politics/04SCOT.html?pagewanted=all.

8. Greenhouse, "Black Robes."

9. Rosaria Butterfield, quoted in Sam Allberry, Rosaria Butterfield, and Christopher Yuan, "Singleness, Same-Sex Attraction, and the Church: A Conversation with Sam Allberry, Rosaria Butterfield,

and Christopher Yuan," *9 Marks* (blog), March 20, 2017, www
.9marks.org/article/singleness-same-sex-attraction-and-the-church
-a-conversation-with-sam-allberry-rosaria-butterfield-and
-christopher-yuan.

Chapter 7: Distinguishing People from Ideas

1. John Gresham Machen, *What Is Christianity?* (Grand Rapids, MI:
    Eerdmans, 1951), 162.

2. J. P. Moreland, *Scientism and Secularism: Learning to Respond to a
    Dangerous Ideology* (Wheaton, IL: Crossway, 2018), 30.

3. Christopher Hitchens, *God Is Not Great: How Religion Poisons
    Everything* (New York: Hachette, 2007), 8.

4. Jason Caine, personal conversation with author.

5. Nadia Suleman, "Young Americans Are Increasingly 'Uncomfort-
    able' with LGBTQ Community, GLAAD Study Shows," *Time,*
    June 25, 2019, https://time.com/5613276/glaad-acceptance-index
    -lgbtq-survey.

6. "Glaad Accelerating Acceptance 2019 Executive Summary: A
    Survey of American Acceptance and Attitudes Toward LGBTQ
    Americans," Harris Poll, 2, www.glaad.org/sites/default/files/
    Accelerating%20Acceptance%202019.pdf.

7. Barack Obama, quoted in Ed Mazza, "Barack Obama Calls Out
    Woke Culture and Twitter Outrage: 'That's Not Activism,'" *Huff-
    ington Post,* October 30, 2019, www.huffpost.com/entry/barack
    -obama-twitter-activism_n_5db9292ee4b0bb1ea3716bb7.

8. Obama, quoted in Mazza, "Barack Obama."

9. Arthur C. Brooks, *Love Your Enemies: How Decent People Can
    Save America from the Culture of Contempt* (New York: Harper-
    Collins, 2019), 14.

10. Martin Luther King Jr., *Strength to Love* (Minneapolis: Fortress,
    2010), 46.

11. Martin Luther King Jr., "Remaining Awake Through a Great
    Revolution" speech, National Cathedral, Washington, DC,
    March 31, 1968, https://kinginstitute.stanford.edu/king-papers/
    publications/knock-midnight-inspiration-great-sermons-reverend
    -martin-luther-king-jr-10.

12. Maya Angelou, *Letter to My Daughter* (New York: Random House, 2008), 149.

13. King Jr., "Remaining Awake."

Chapter 8: Helping Others Think Empathetically

1. Ralph Waldo Emerson, "The Over-Soul," in *The Complete Essays and Other Writings of Ralph Waldo Emerson* (New York: Modern Library, 1950), 261.

2. Sam Harris, *The Moral Landscape: How Science Can Determine Human Values* (New York: Free Press, 2010), 147.

3. Sam Harris, *Letter to a Christian Nation* (New York: Vintage, 2008), 26.

4. Arthur C. Brooks, *Love Your Enemies: How Decent People Can Save America from the Culture of Contempt* (New York: Harper-Collins, 2019), 210.

5. "Feminist Speaks Out Against Trans Movement," YouTube video, 4:02, posted by "Fox News," February 12, 2019, www.youtube.com/watch?v=aQns3VsYdd4&t=100s.

6. Howard Hendricks and William Hendricks, *Living by the Book: The Art and Science of Reading the Bible* (Chicago: Moody, 2007), 43.

7. Melissa M. Wilcox, "When Sheila's a Lesbian: Religious Individualism Among Lesbian, Gay, Bisexual, and Transgender Christians," *Sociology of Religion,* 63 no. 4 (Winter 2002), 505.

8. Dr. Henry Cloud, *Integrity: The Courage to Meet the Demands of Reality* (New York: HarperCollins, 2006), 56.

Chapter 9: Do You Have the Credibility to Walk with Others?

1. Brian Buxton, "This Sermon Changed My Life," *J. D. Greear Ministries* (blog), July 11, 2016, https://jdgreear.com/blog/the-sermon-that-changed-my-life.

2. Buxton, "This Sermon."

3. Dr. Henry Cloud, *Integrity: The Courage to Meet the Demands of Reality* (New York: HarperCollins, 2006), 24.

4. Andy Stanley, *Louder Than Words: The Power of Uncompromised Living* (Colorado Springs: Multnomah, 2004), 31.

5. Nicholas Sparks, *The Last Song* (New York: Grand Central, 2009), 149.

6. Stanley, *Louder,* 28.

7. Helen Keller, Brainy Quote, www.brainyquote.com/quotes/helen_keller_101340.

8. Dusty Frizzell, personal conversation with author.

9. Thomas Paine, Brainy Quote, www.brainyquote.com/quotes/thomas_paine_106084.

10. Kerry Patterson, *Crucial Conversations: Tools for Talking When Stakes Are High* (New York: McGraw-Hill, 2012), 35.

11. For more information, see Daniel J. Simons and Christopher F. Chabris, "Gorillas in Our Midst: Sustained Inattentional Blindness for Dynamic Events," *Perception* 28, no. 9 (1999): 1065.

12. Paul David Tripp, *Instruments in the Redeemer's Hands: People in Need of Change Helping People in Need of Change,* Resources for Changing Lives (Phillipsburg, NJ: P&R, 2002), 209.

13. Scott Sauls, *Befriend: Create Belonging in an Age of Judgment, Isolation, and Fear* (Carol Stream, IL: Tyndale, 2016), 3.

14. Tyler Chernesky, "Four Ways to Build Lasting Friendships," *Tyler Chernesky* (blog), January 26, 2019, www.tylerchernesky.com/post/buildfriendships.

15. Andy Stanley, "Five Reasons People Leave the Church," *Fox News,* September 23, 2018, www.foxnews.com/opinion/five-reasons-people-leave-the-church.

16. Rusty George, *Justice. Mercy. Humility: A Simple Path to Following Jesus* (Bloomington, MN: Bethany, 2019), 132.

17. Timothy Keller, quoted in Julius J. Kim, *Preaching the Whole Counsel of God: Design and Deliver Gospel-Centered Sermons* (Grand Rapids, MI: Zondervan, 2015), 64.

Chapter 10: Prioritizing and Preparing for Dialogue

1. Brené Brown, *Daring Greatly: How the Courage to Be Vulnerable Transforms the Way We Live, Love, Parent, and Lead* (New York: Avery, 2015), 81.

2. Mark A. Yarhouse, "Sexual Orientation and Identity," in *Sanctified Sexuality: Valuing Sex in an Oversexed World,* ed. Sandra L. Glahn and C. Gary Barnes (Grand Rapids, MI: Kregel, 2020), 315.

3. Jackie Hill Perry, *Gay Girl, Good God: The Story of Who I Was, and Who God Has Always Been* (Nashville: Broadman, Holman, 2018), 69.

4. Harriet Beecher Stowe, quoted in Susan Ratcliffe, *Oxford Essential Quotations* (Oxford University Press, 2016), www.oxfordreference.com/view/10.1093/acref/9780191826719.001.0001/q-oro-ed4-00010502.

5. Dr. Henry Cloud and Dr. John Townsend, *How to Have That Difficult Conversation You've Been Avoiding* (Grand Rapids, MI: Zondervan, 2005), 38.

6. Karen M. Staller, "Difficult Conversations: Talking *with* Rather Than Talking *At*," *Qualitative Social Work* 13, no. 2 (March 7, 2014): 172.

Chapter 11: Difficult Conversations That Don't Destroy

1. Henry Wasonga Abuto, "Oriented to Love: How to Dialogue in the Midst of Great Differences," *An Unconventional Life* (blog), August 13, 2019, www.henryabuto.com/blog/oq8d3pyvo5ly8tubdhnqeokjsrqoqv-22r7f.

2. Abuto, "Oriented to Love."

3. Rusty George with Michael DeFazio, *When You, Then God: 7 Things God Is Waiting to Do in Your Life* (Carol Stream, IL: Tyndale, 2016), 165.

4. Dr. Henry Cloud, *The Power of the Other: The Startling Effect Other People Have on You, from the Boardroom to the Bedroom and Beyond—and What to Do About It* (New York: HarperCollins, 2016), 118–19.

5. John Ortberg, *Everybody's Normal till You Get to Know Them* (Grand Rapids, MI: Zondervan, 2003), 181.

6. Darrell L. Bock and Mikel Del Rosario, "The Table Briefing: Leading with Courage and Compassion," *Bibliotheca Sacra* 176 (January–March 2019): 96.

7. Miroslav Volf, *A Public Faith: How Followers of Christ Should Serve the Common Good* (Grand Rapids, MI: Brazos Press, 2011), 126.

8. Rosaria Champagne Butterfield, *The Secret Thoughts of an Unlikely Convert: An English Professor's Journey into Christian Faith* (Pittsburgh: Crown and Covenant, 2014), 21–22.

9. Timothy Keller, *Prayer: Experiencing Awe and Intimacy with God* (New York: Penguin Books, 2014), 228.

10. Howard Hendricks, *Teaching to Change Lives: Seven Proven Ways to Make Your Teaching Come Alive* (Colorado Springs: Multnomah, 2003), 35.

11. John C. Maxwell, *Good Leaders Ask Great Questions* (New York: Hachette, 2014), 59.

12. Darrell L. Bock, "How to Make Ethical Decisions," in *Sanctified Sexuality: Valuing Sex in an Oversexed World*, ed. Sandra L. Glahn and C. Gary Barnes (Grand Rapids, MI: Kregel, 2020), 350.

13. Dr. Henry Cloud and Dr. John Townsend, *How to Have That Difficult Conversation You've Been Avoiding* (Grand Rapids, MI: Zondervan, 2005), 44.

Chapter 12: Are You a Guide or a Gatekeeper?

1. Caleb Kaltenbach, *Messy Grace: How a Pastor with Gay Parents Learned to Love Others Without Sacrificing Conviction* (Colorado Springs: WaterBrook, 2015), 158.

2. J. P. Moreland, *Kingdom Triangle: Recover the Christian Mind, Renovate the Soul, Restore the Spirit's Power* (Grand Rapids, MI: Zondervan, 2007), 26.

3. Carey Nieuwhof, *Didn't See It Coming: Overcoming the 7 Greatest Challenges That No One Expects and Everyone Experiences* (Colorado Springs: WaterBrook, 2018), 167.

4. Donald Miller, *Building a StoryBrand: Clarify Your Message So*

Customers Will Listen (Nashville: HarperCollins Leadership, 2017), 77.

5. Dusty Frizzell, "The Power of One: The Captain and His Ship," May 26, 2019, in *Shepherd Church Sermon Podcast,* Himalaya video, 35:00, www.himalaya.com/christianity-podcasts/shepherd -church-sermon-podcast-958927/the-power-of-one-the-captain -and-his-ship-60146939.

6. Christopher Yuan, "Why 'God and the Gay Christian' Is Wrong About the Bible and Same-Sex Relationships," *Christianity Today,* June 9, 2014, www.christianitytoday.com/ct/2014/june-web-only/ why-matthew-vines-is-wrong-about-bible-same-sex-relationshi .html.

7. Ed Stetzer, *Christians in the Age of Outrage: How to Bring Our Best When the World Is at Its Worst* (Carol Stream, IL: Tyndale, 2018), 260.

8. Richard J. Mouw, *When the Kings Come Marching In: Isaiah and the New Jerusalem* (Grand Rapids, MI: Eerdmans, 2002), 86.

READING LIST

An increasing number of books are being released that engage sexuality and faith. These books contain personal testimonies, a variety of perspectives, examinations of different theological aspects of sexuality, and so on. The following is a list of books that echo some of the principles and beliefs in *Messy Truth*. While the following authors and I may disagree on some topics, their work would still add immense value to your life.

Allberry, Sam. *7 Myths About Singleness*. Wheaton, IL: Crossway, 2019.

———. *Why Does God Care Who I Sleep With?* Epsom, Surrey, England: Good Book, 2020.

Bennett, David. *A War of Loves: The Unexpected Story of a Gay Activist Discovering Jesus*. Grand Rapids, MI: Zondervan, 2018.

Butterfield, Rosaria Champagne. *Openness Unhindered: Further Thoughts of an Unlikely Convert on Sexual Identity and Union with Christ*. Pittsburgh: Crown and Covenant, 2015.

Cloud, Dr. Henry, and Dr. John Townsend. *How to Have That Difficult Conversation: Gaining the Skills for Honest and Meaningful Communication*. Grand Rapids, MI: Zondervan, 2015.

Coles, Gregory. *No Longer Strangers: Finding Belonging in a World of Alienation*. Downer's Grove, IL: IVP, 2021.

Cook, Becket. *A Change of Affection: A Gay Man's Incredible Story of Redemption*. Nashville: Thomas Nelson, 2019.

Gilson, Rachel. *Born Again This Way: Coming Out, Coming to Faith, and What Comes Next*. Epsom, Surrey, England: Good Book, 2020.

Glahn, Sandra L., and C. Gary Barnes, eds. *Sanctified Sexuality: Valuing Sex in an Oversexed World*. Grand Rapids, MI: Kregel, 2020.

Harlow, Tim. *What Made Jesus Mad? Rediscover the Blunt, Sarcastic, Passionate Savior of the Bible*. Nashville: Thomas Nelson, 2019.

Joiner, Reggie, Kristen Ivy, and Tom Shefchunas. *When Relationships Matter: Make Your Church a Place where Kids and Teenagers Belong*. Cumming, GA: Orange Books, 2019.

McDowell, Sean. *Chasing Love: Sex, Love, and Relationships in a Confused Culture*. Nashville: B&H Publishing, 2020.

McLaughlin, Rebecca. *Confronting Christianity: 12 Hard Questions for the World's Largest Religion*. Wheaton, IL: Crossway, 2019.

Patterson, Kerry, Joseph Grenny, Ron McMillan, and Al Switzler. *Crucial Conversations: Tools for Talking When Stakes Are High*. New York: McGraw-Hill, 2012.

Perry, Jackie Hill. *Gay Girl, Good God*. Nashville: Broadman, Holman, 2018.

Sauls, Scott. *A Gentle Answer: Our "Secret Weapon" in an Age of Us Against Them*. Nashville: Thomas Nelson, 2020.

Slattery, Dr. Juli. *Rethinking Sexuality: God's Design and Why It Matters*. Colorado Springs: Multnomah, 2018.

Sprinkle, Preston. *Embodied: Transgender Identities, the Church, and What the Bible Has to Say*. Colorado Springs: David C Cook, 2021.

Stanley, Andy. *Better Decisions, Fewer Regrets: 5 Questions to Help You Determine Your Next Move*. Grand Rapids, MI: Zondervan, 2020.

Stetzer, Ed. *Christians in the Age of Outrage: How to Bring Our Best When the World Is at Its Worst*. Carol Stream, IL: Tyndale, 2018.

Welcher, Rachel Joy. *Talking Back to Purity Culture: Rediscovering Faithful Christian Sexuality*. Downer's Grove, IL: InterVarsity, 2020.

Yarhouse, Mark, and Julia Sadusky. *Emerging Gender Identities: Under-*

standing the Diverse Experiences of Today's Youth. Grand Rapids, MI: Brazos Press, 2020.

Yuan, Christopher. *Holy Sexuality and the Gospel: Sex, Desire, and Relationships Shaped by God's Grand Story.* Colorado Springs: Multnomah, 2018.

Caleb Kaltenbach is a pastor and the author of *Messy Grace* and *God of Tomorrow*. Through the Messy Grace Group, he helps leaders, Christian organizations, and churches develop influence with LGBTQ individuals without sacrificing theological convictions. He's a graduate of Ozark Christian College, Talbot School of Theology at Biola University, and he received his doctorate from Dallas Theological Seminary. A frequent speaker on faith, sexuality, and society, Caleb has been a guest on or contributed to the *New York Times, Fox and Friends, Christianity Today,* the *Carey Nieuwhof Leadership Podcast, Christian Standard, Focus on the Family,* and more. He and his family live in Southern California and practically live at Disneyland. You can find out more about Caleb and his ministry at calebkaltenbach.com and messygracegroup.org.